THE FRESH TABLE

Louisiana State University Press)|(Baton Rouge

— THE —
FRESH TABLE

COOKING IN
LOUISIANA
ALL YEAR ROUND

HELANA BRIGMAN

Published by Louisiana State University Press
Copyright © 2013 by Louisiana State University Press
All rights reserved
Manufactured in the United States of America
First printing

Designer: Barbara Neely Bourgoyne
Typefaces: Verb and Whitman
Printer and binder: Thomson-Shore, Inc.

Library of Congress Cataloging-in-Publication Data
Brigman, Helana, 1986–
    The fresh table : cooking in Louisiana all year round / Helana Brigman.
        pages cm
    Includes index.
    ISBN 978-0-8071-5046-7 (cloth : alk. paper) — ISBN 978-0-8071-5047-4 (pdf) —
ISBN 978-0-8071-5048-1 (epub) — ISBN 978-0-8071-5049-8 (mobi) 1. Cooking,
American—Louisiana style. 2. Cookbooks. lcgft I. Title.
    TX715.2.L68B76 2013
    641.59763—dc23
                                                        2012039076

For Linda and Lise

Contents

Acknowledgments

WRITING A COOKBOOK is a labor of love, a compilation of experiences in appetite and life. In these pages I have collated close to a hundred moments of modern Louisiana cookery and culture, and it is not without the dedication of many minds and stomachs that *The Fresh Table* has been actualized. Although I have been privileged to cook with and for a multitude of Louisiana residents, it is a daunting task to catalogue the number of people who made these moments so special, but here is a certain list.

The Fresh Table would not have been possible without the endless support and help of Alisa Plant, acquisitions editor and editor of food and foodways at LSU Press. The LSU Press family—in particular MaryKatherine Callaway, Barbara Neely Bourgoyne, and Neal Novak—and its creative and editorial departments have been beyond wonderful (especially Jo Ann Kiser and her fantastic copyedits). I am thrilled my first book is with such an institution of Louisiana publishing and culture.

Stephanie Riegel for a little article on Baton Rouge food bloggers and bringing me on as part of the Food section at *The Advocate*. Cheramie Sonnier for continuing her support of my column, "Fresh Ideas," and for the endless tips and tricks in my recipe writing. Beth Colvin for making me laugh and giving me access to the Advocate's test kitchen.

Jon Barry for your photography, fellowship, and mentor-like wisdom.

Russ Turley for your laughter, enthusiasm, and wonderful rapport.

Lydia Dorsey for eating everything I make and always making me laugh. Dennis "Bruno" Wiggins for more than one brunch at The Chimes and your potent cocktails. Laura Keigan and Christina Janke for your hungry stomachs and recipe enthusiasm. Jessica and Victor Pineda for being the best of foodie friends and Rhett Clement for helping me in more than one cooking undertaking, making me smile, and tasting so many of my dishes. Carol Pegues Dorsey for first introducing me to Silpats (and many other kitchen gadgets).

Rosemary Peters and Shannon Kipping Caldwell, whose personal soup recipes made it into this book although in variation. *The Fresh Table* would not be the same without "Rosemary's Rosemary Pumpkin Soup" and Shannon's "Cleo's Oyster Artichoke Soup." I'm grateful to both friends for such wonderfully inspirational content, and Shannon, especially, for sharing the story of her grandmother's New Orleans.

Other indispensable stomachs—Kris and Ellen Mecholsky (and Eliza and Mathilda!) for four years of fabulous meals together, John Edgar Browning and Michael Agan for some wonderful memories and recipes, Lauren Pendas for much needed girl time and pizza, Tara Beth Smithson for everything juice-related, Andrew Hill for a certain Strawberry Cake birthday, Marion Cotillons for showing me how the French make *real* crêpes, and Peter Pappas for his good taste, friendship, and skillfully voracious male appetite.

Close family and friends—Haley Dawn Jones and Lise, Paul, Caroline, and Peter Duda for our Christmas Bouillabaisse and a childhood of cookies. Linda Jones for teaching me so much about cooking and always letting me make a mess in her kitchen.

A big thanks to my mother, Rebecca Brigman, who always took great pleasure in cooking for others. I watched and learned from this pleasure enormously, and I know that I have internalized this approach to cooking somehow. Although gone, you are never forgotten, and I like to believe I'm just a little closer to you with the recipes that fill these pages. Christmas morning would never have been the same without your Red Beans and Rice or New England Fish and Clam Chowder.

Finally, my mentors in the LSU English department—Sharon Aronofsky Weltman, Robert Hamm, and Dan Novak. I realize it's rare for a doctoral candidate to publish, cook, and pursue writing careers outside of the ivory towers while still working on her dissertation, but I must give many thanks for all of the support and guidance you've given me as I've taken this time to write and publish.

Last, but not least, I dedicate my book not to a famous Louisiana chef or gastronome, but to two of my favorite dinner companions, Lise Duda and Linda Jones. Thank you for every piece of guidance and opportunity for exploration in your kitchens. Every time I cook and eat, I continue to be inspired by your wise, loving, and fantastic culinary presences both then and now. Let us all cook, eat, and drink whatever the season.

Thank you all.

THE FRESH TABLE

INTRODUCTION

ANYONE WHO HAS spent time in Louisiana is susceptible to falling in love with its charms—the incredible weather, music, carnival season, and definitely the food. Unlike many states, Louisiana's heat warms some of the South's best produce, creating a hot bed for ruby red tomatoes, strawberries, and watermelons in summer months and for root vegetables, citrus, and gourds in the winter ones. With southern Louisiana's access to the Gulf and its rich Cajun-Creole heritage, Louisiana markets and cooking traditions represent a magical blend of new and old approaches to cooking that have created for many homes a fresh table.

Although I was born in New Orleans, I didn't spend my childhood in the South and it wasn't until my twenties that I returned to the state expecting to master the skills necessary for my mother's gumbo, dirty rice, étouffée, and jambalaya. With my increased exposure to Louisiana kitchens, I realized that these dishes may be the posted menu items of many residents, but the concepts and ingredients have continued to evolve into newer, and yes, *fresher* forms.

In 2008, I launched the Web site Clearly Delicious—a food, cooking, and recipe travel blog. Although I could not have anticipated at the time that my most popular recipes would not be traditional Louisiana fare, but new takes on old favorites, I knew there was something worth pursuing in the local markets and menus of our Louisiana homes. Recipes that seek the flavor of Louisiana cooking have always been my core content, and it is in these early test samples presented at Clearly Delicious that my views on fresh seasonal Louisiana dishes have been formed.

This is not to say that many local chefs don't grace their families with tried and true dishes from their parents' repertoire, but rather that aspects unique to Louisiana cooking demand some reconfiguration. I suspect that most Louisiana chefs are like me, seeing traditional meat items like Boudin as not-so-surprising assets to our everyday cooking. Whether it's a breakfast omelet or dinnertime spicy pizza, this Cajun "sausage" has evolved as part of new practices in increasingly modernized kitchens. Whether it's the way we serve watermelon—not just from the rind, but now, as a juice—or the way we cook steak—dolloped in fresh herb butter—Louisiana cooking evokes the flavors of its traditions, but in exciting new forms. Simultaneously, with the popularity of farmers' markets, the availability of locally grown produce, and the increasing interest in slow food movements, what appears on Louisiana tables could not be more exciting for local gastronomes.

The concept here is really quite simple: in perhaps one of the most unique states in cookery culture, Louisiana tables are discovering modern takes on classic ingredients alongside some beautifully fresh produce. I have endeavored to give voice to this shifting tradition in the recipe banks that follow so that home chefs might develop a feel for the classic ingredients of Louisiana cooking while experiencing these ingredients when they are at their peak of freshness. To eat seasonally provides the main focus of the recipes listed in this book, but I also hope the message of eating *locally* inspires readers as well.

For me, these approaches to *The Fresh Table* reflect the ways in which culinary traditions in Louisiana are shifting naturally while also giving voice to how I approach cooking daily. What's affordable, fresh, and available for many home chefs determines in every season what you'll find on our tables.

HOW TO USE THIS BOOK

Online Components—Clearly Delicious and Food Blogging

The birth of *The Fresh Table: Cooking in Louisiana All Year Round* happened online. And once having mastered the recipes in this book, readers may find further instruction, recipe ideas, and step-by-step photos continued there. Clearly Delicious, my food, cooking, and recipe travel blog, like the food blogs popularized in movies such as *Julie & Julia,* connects daily recipes to readers—and hungry tummies—in an instant educational format. Many of the recipes produced in this book began in earlier posts online, whereas others have been newly created for this volume. Since space limits me from showing each step in visual detail or offering further tantalizing photos, readers can expect an interactive online experience as they look (and cook) through these pages.

When writing *The Fresh Table: Cooking in Louisiana All Year Round,* I paid close attention both to seasonal availability and to the availability of our time. Most cooking enthusiasts will tell you they wish they had the opportunity to bake their own bread, roast their own peppers, grow their own herbs, and, well, do just about everything supermarkets make accessible for the seasonal chef. As a result, recipes in this book are set up to save time as much as possible while not sacrificing the quality of a dish or its seasonal resources. For example, I suggest using store-bought roasted red peppers in my Summer Gazpacho with Avocado and Cucumbers (Summer), or precooked lasagna sheets when pressing ravioli for both my Pumpkin Sage Ravioli (Autumn) and my Crawfish Étouffée Ravioli with Spicy Cream Sauce (Summer). Although many cooks recognize the amount of flavor to be gained when we prepare raw ingredients ourselves, one of the benefits of cooking as modern chefs in Louisiana comes from just how accessible certain alternative ingredients can be. At Clearly Delicious, I offer alternatives to many of my recipes in the same ways listed above. But, the more enthusiastic chef with available time may find homemade instructions as well.

For those of us who find the time—and often, the pleasure—to perform the homemade tasks outlined above, see "Stocking Your Pantry" for explanatory notes on the best kitchen tools and equipment to have at your disposal, the cooking techniques discussed in this book, and of course, the not-so-short-cuts to preparing certain dishes from scratch.

One of my greatest passions in the preparation of food is the art of plating it. Often only enjoyed for the quick moments a dinner companion looks down upon my cooking, beautiful food often disappears as quickly as it is arranged. One might argue that I turned to food photography as a way of immortalizing these brief moments—that is, the moment of anticipation, right before the meal is consumed. Hungry eyes know that food must be good simply because it *looks* amazing, and I am constantly inspired to represent this stage of the eating and cooking process. It is my hope that readers of *The Fresh Table* may find enjoyment in the often close-up, always brightly colored images of the food prepared within this book, as well as online. For me, and in fact, for you, these moments of anticipation might excite you into trying certain recipes while ensuring that just how delicious a meal may look can, in fact, remain for more than a moment, but for every season.

Spring through Winter: Appetizers, Entrées, Side Dishes, Desserts, Lagniappe

The recipes in *The Fresh Table* offer a wide menu of appetizers, soups, salads, entrées, desserts, breakfasts, and "other" items (the something extra Louisianans call "Lagniappe"). Most take a cue from the fruits and vegetables best prepared during their respective season, whereas others evoke the demands for a cooling cocktail on a hot summer day or the warming powers of soup in winter months.

At the end of this book, I have suggested a list of possible menus for each season, combining recipes from appetizers to desserts. Additionally, I have included a more standard index of recipes based on their category instead of their season.

APPETIZERS: Flavorful starters begin each section, prepared from ripe avocadoes (Summer), seasonal beets (Winter), sweet Pea Pesto (Spring), and Candied Dates with Cheese and Prosciutto (Autumn). Other appetizers invite guests to dig into Perfect Guacamole in the Summer, nibble on Bourbon Candied Pecans in the Winter and to savor smaller, more *amuse-bouche* starters such as bite-size slices of Asian Pears with Honey, Gorgonzola Cheese, and Bourbon Candied Pecans in Autumn. Each season offers a wide variety of the savory and sweet introduced best at the beginning of fresh meals.

ENTRÉES: Main courses delve into the more modern branches of Cajun and Creole cooking with crawfish, duck, sirloin steak, oysters, shrimp, and chicken. Whether it's Pumpkin-Encrusted Chicken Parmesan (Autumn), Cajun Bouillabaisse (Winter), or Fig and Prosciutto Pizza (Summer), seasonal availability shows just how much fresh ingredients can bring a beautiful roast, steak, or bed of pasta to life. Traditional Cajun-Creole spices infuse recognized flavors into everyday meals in a way that only Louisiana cooking can.

SIDE DISHES: More than just plate fillers, side dishes highlight the rich varieties for preparing locally grown produce. Red Pepper Aioli drizzled on Artichokes (Spring), sweet summer Corn tossed with Black Bean Salsa (Summer), and Spiced Sweet Potatoes flavored with almonds (Autumn) recommend just some of the ways side dishes may be as interesting as their main courses.

DESSERTS: Perhaps the arena that has undergone the most change is desserts. Dessert items may look like your grandmother's Banana Pudding, but they add innovating alternatives (see the suggested addition of Biscoff cookies along with simple vanilla wafers in this Summer dish). Pumpkin Spice Bread Pudding (Autumn) and Pomegranate Christmas Cake with Snow-White Cream Cheese Icing (Winter) create the background of seasonal cooking inspired by nature itself.

LAGNIAPPE: Brunch, snack items, bread, and beverages offer some extra opportunities to incorporate the seasons into everyday eating. Consider Warm Abita Molasses Bread (Winter), Lemonade with Strawberries or Limes (Summer), and Bananas Foster Croissant French Toast (Spring).

STOCKING YOUR PANTRY
What to Use and How to Use It

I ONCE HAD a friend tell me that he couldn't help but marvel at the amount of spices, sauces, and gadgets in my kitchen: "You just have everything you could possibly need to cook with. I feel like I'm always spending money on some ingredient I only use once when I'm trying something new. Buying ingredients is *expensive*," he whined.

I must admit, his point was well taken. It's difficult to know as a new chef exactly what tools or ingredients you'll need in your kitchen and how often you might expect to use them. Fortunately, Louisiana cooking offers some wonderful guidelines on what and how these devices will suit your cooking needs. I outline here a list of the spices, fresh herbs, olive oils, and other more general ingredients I have on hand all year round, along with the produce I suggest having readily available when the weather is particularly hot (such as lemons, limes, and avocados) or particularly cold (such as broth for stews and soups). Other homemade suggestions fill the next few pages on what we can make at home easily and freeze or keep on hand—homemade pasta (if you're into that sort of thing), homemade pizza dough, roasted red peppers, and several other ideas for the seasonal chef.

Throughout *The Fresh Table,* I will make mention of specific tools, equipment, and gadgets that are necessary for certain recipes. Many cooks may find that they already have the same or overlapping items, but for those who may need substitutes, I suggest alternative variations throughout. Read the "Kitchen Tools/ Equipment List" below for a specific outlining of what my kitchen entails and the "Useful Substitutions for Missing Equipment List" for ways to get around the absence of certain gadgets.

Kitchen Tools and Equipment List: Suggested Tools and Equipment from My Own Kitchen

COFFEE GRINDER: At first glance, a coffee grinder may seem ill placed on such a list as I have no recipes for coffee in this book. Yet, the perks of a coffee grinder are that it does just that—*grinds*. Grinding will come up throughout the course of these recipes as a tool you'll want to have easily available. The grinding of lavender for my Blueberry Balsamic Gelato (Summer) or Lemon Lavender Muffins (Spring) occurs more than once, but so do the grinding of other herbs and almond meals.

ICE CREAM MAKER: Modern kitchen appliances today make the preparing of your own ice cream and gelato extremely easy. Unlike the hand-churned contraptions of the past that involved crushing ice into a dairy mixture (to create the "ice" part of your "cream"), modern ice cream makers generate a silky smooth frozen dessert with very little work. I suggest the Cuisinart brand here as it's what has worked wonderfully in my kitchen for the Blueberry Balsamic Gelato recipe found in the Summer section. However, if another fully automatic two- or four-quart brand is at your disposal, by all means use it.

CRÊPE PAN: This flatiron pan is designed for crêpes specifically. The microscopic bubbles of the enamel's nonstick finish make the even heating of crêpe batter a kind of scientific wonder in the kitchen. Although you can still make crêpes with a nonstick skillet, the results may be more pancake-y and less even. Here, I suggest this proper tool for quality purposes. I use and recommend the crêpe pans made by Le Creuset.

FOOD PROCESSOR: Hands down, one of the most useful and multifunctional items on this list is a universal food processor. Although many home chefs can substitute a blender for certain processing needs, food processors really make food preparation superbly easy with their sharp spinning blades for grating, chopping, pulsing, and pureeing. I use my processor weekly for everything from my Sundried Tomato Hummus (Autumn) to converting graham crackers to crumbs as with my crust for Raspberry Almond Cream Cheese Tartlets (Summer). Whether it's making pesto, dips, or other moist items, a processor can perform traditionally handheld tasks in a way that saves time more than any other gadget (perhaps with

exception of similar attachments that may be available with a KitchenAid mixer). Here, I don't suggest any particular brand, but I do suggest a middle-to-upper grade quality processor, as they will often last longer.

JUICER: Used here mostly in the preparation of Watermelon Juice with Basil (Summer), a standard electronic juicer speedily prepares cold fruit and vegetable beverages. My favorite aspect of electronic juicers is how, with watermelon, they juice the entire fruit so long as you refeed the leftover pulp through the fruit feeder until entirely depleted. Affordable (usually not more than $30), this appliance *does* get used in my experience. Other ways to plan on using your juicer may be with the processing of fresh ripe tomatoes for tomato juice as with my Bloody Marys the Louisiana way (Summer).

LEMON SQUEEZER (HANDHELD): As time goes by, I have learned that not much beats a simple handheld lemon squeezer. The unique half-lemon shape developed specifically for the juicing of citrus prevents seeds and pulp from fogging fresh lemon juice by straining fruit as you squeeze the handles together. Although electronic juicers are indispensible when juicing most fruits, handheld squeezers for citrus are the right tool for any lemon/lime/orange juice job.

MIXER AND ATTACHMENTS—DOUGH HOOK, WHISK, AND PADDLE: A great mixer is indispensable. In particular, a KitchenAid mixer suggests a chef who is serious about cooking. More than just a simple hands-free mixer, this device offers restaurant-grade quality to recipes prepared in the home. Rarely do I endorse specific brands, but there's a reason why KitchenAid is as popular today as it was when my mother was cooking. Because of the quality of the brand's kitchen appliances, you can expect your one-time purchase to last for years to come.

In my kitchen, this mixer finds a way into every dessert, batter, or dough I make. Whether it's kneading simple pizza doughs for ten minutes with the dough hook or beating meringue with the whisk attachment, the mixer does extraordinary amounts of work for you with precision. Plus, the company is always improving upon attachments that make every part of cooking fun.

MEZZALUNA: Tired of pizza cutting wheels that slip, slide, and just aren't sharp enough when slicing through pizza dough? Try a Mezzaluna—a semi-circular blade with two handles—that makes the cutting of pizza fun and effective. I love my Mezzaluna if only for the effort and time it saves me when cutting pizza slices. Whereas an American pizza wheel requires the energy and pressure of one hand, a Mezzaluna uses both hands to push back and forth in a simple slicing technique. Also useful for the chopping of herbs and vegetables, this uniquely shaped knife is an addictive purchase.

MORTAR AND PESTLE: A fantastic duo tool that works best for crushing pomegranate seeds, herbs, or pastes or simply mashing together a large batch of guacamole. If used for its crushing purposes, a mortar and pestle's heavy stone (or wood) materials make many aspects of food preparation effortless. For my kitchen, I use a heavy-duty stone mortar and pestle with built-in natural stone texture to aid in crushing processes. Some chefs prefer wooden variations of this tool, but I always find that they become grimy over time whereas stone ones can be wiped perfectly clean.

MULTI-FACE GRATER: Most chefs already have some kind of grater in their kitchens, but I wanted to take a moment to point out how graters will be employed in this book. Several times I make mention to the cutting of meats and vegetables "carpaccio" style—an Italian word that literally means to cut something as thinly as possible. Carpaccio food preparation can be made easy with a simple at-home grater that has a flat blade on its side. Most chefs forget the side blades exist on standard graters, but they come in most handy when preparing the thinly cut zucchini for my Summer Pasta Salad with Zucchini, Almonds, and Goat Cheese or even the watermelon radishes for my Watermelon Radish Crostini with Butter and Sea Salt in the same section. As for size and structure, box-style graters of the four-sided variety are actually somewhat dangerous and account for many of the nicks and cuts your hands undergo in grater-related food preparation. More complex-looking graters with six or eight sides remedy the stability issues of a four-sided grater while also offering a whole host of new single blades that cut, grate, and shred.

PIZZA STONE: Better than any kind of cookie sheet or circular pie pan you might own, a simple $10 pizza stone heats dough evenly and, over time, will contribute to the flavor of your dish. The technology here relies on the simple firebrick stone materials most often used in their manufacturing. By using firebrick stone, homemade pizzas develop the same flavors as those from traditional pizza ovens, which are often lined in firebrick. Although this kitchen item can most definitely be skipped when shopping for your kitchen, it's a good one-time investment—as this stone *won't* crack with changing temperatures and does absorb unnecessary moisture when baking—that will make any homemade pizza just a little bit gourmet. Stones may also be used for yeast breads, biscuits, and flat breads like focaccia for added flavor.

SILPAT: A nonstick mat used much like wax paper, a Silpat will be mentioned at times when it is not best to put your food directly on a baking sheet. Woven from a combination of silicone and glass, Silpats are great for baking, rolling, and warming food in the oven. See my recipe for Strawberry Pavlova (Spring) for ways Silpats prevent the burning of foods, or use one whenever making scones or biscuits.

STEAMING BASKET: One of the best ways to prepare fresh vegetables is not just through roasting or grilling, but steaming in water or other poaching liquids. Metal steaming baskets come in a variety of sizes usually ranging from 9 to 11 inches. Simply fold down the perforated basket into a pot of water, broth, or other liquid, and fill with vegetables for steaming, as with my Artichokes with Red Pepper Aioli (Spring). You can also use this tool for steaming fish and meats as

it's one of the simplest ways to cook without adding many calories to a dish.

TART SHELLS: Unlike cake pans, tart shells create unique molds for crusts and cakes that offer elegance to bakery items. Truly, this device is for those serious bakers who *will* find themselves making the Glazed Tarte Aux Baies (Spring) or the Chocolate Cake with Red Wine Pears (Autumn) in this book. I have a standard 10-inch circular tart pan with a removable bottom that I use regularly. For individual tarts, readers can invest in 4-inch diameter ones for making my Raspberry Almond Cream Cheese Tartlets or Key Lime Cheesecake Tarts (both found in Summer).

(SUGGESTED) KNIVES: Here, I opt not to suggest a specific brand, but to advocate for the *kinds* of knives every kitchen should have. A good chef's knife, bread knife, paring knife, filet knife, serrated steak knife, and of course, a knife sharpener are paramount to any cooking endeavor. Chefs who find themselves working with large quantities of meat should ensure owning a serious meat cleaver, whereas bakers who finely chop chocolate or nuts regularly should always own a quality chef's knife. Ranging in size based on purpose—a chef's knife can be 6 to 10 inches, whereas a paring knife may not exceed 4 inches. Here, the important concept is to pick a good quality stainless steel knife that can be easily sharpened and maintained. What brand you select really comes down to buyer's choice since there are endless brands that manufacture quality knives. As for maintaining usage, as my friend Russ always says, "a sharp knife is a *safe* knife." I couldn't agree more with this chef's tip.

Essential Food Items and Ingredients: What to Have on Hand All Year Round

BOUDIN: Readers of these recipes may not be surprised that I have a minor love affair with this unique Louisiana dirty rice sausage. Part meat and part rice, Boudin has a creamy quality unique to its makeup with which I can't stop experimenting. Most often served with breakfast, brunch, or grill items, Boudin transcends nicely to various lunchtime sausage sautés and dinner pizzas. As I will continue to be drawn to the versatility of this meat, I am certain Boudin can be used in making everything from a killer panini to a complex Louisiana burger. Most commonly sold as *Boudin blanc*, this gray-colored variety includes pork without the "blood," although more than one chef has told me that *Boudin noir* (Boudin "blood sausage") has significantly more flavor. Readers should use *Boudin blanc* where Boudin is listed.

CAJUN SEASONING: By far one of the most unique salt-based spices in my kitchen, Tony Chachere's Cajun Seasoning combines a heavy dose of salt with Cajun spices like red pepper and garlic. Most Louisiana cookbooks simply advocate the use of "Cajun seasoning" when cooking, but I advocate this brand specifically as it has just the right amount of hot spice and salt. When cooking with Tony's, it's important to re-member that the ingredient should be treated as *salt*. Salt being the primary component of the blend, it is entirely unnecessary to add salt to a dish when cooking with Tony's. I first suggest the ingredient when making my Spinach Artichoke Dip with Spicy Cayenne (Spring) and continue to suggest this ingredient as the salt rim for a Louisiana Bloody Mary (Summer).

CRAWFISH: Perhaps the most iconic seafood in Louisiana, crawfish meat has the savory qualities of lobster with a very different flavor. Like Boudin, I find crawfish is excellent with almost anything so long as your dinner companion is a fan of shellfish. Frozen precooked and shelled crawfish tails are available all over Louisiana (including, yes, the grocery aisles of Wal-Mart), and, so long as frozen *fresh*, pre-prepared crawfish tails save enormous amounts of time in the kitchen. For the recipes in this book, use peeled fresh crawfish tails when available or else fresh frozen crawfish tails.

HERBS SUGGESTED THROUGHOUT (THYME, BASIL, ROSEMARY AND THEIR SUBSEQUENT RECIPES): A healthy reliance on fresh, quality herbs is a must in my kitchen, and I believe that many Louisiana chefs feel similarly about the ways the following herbs work in our cuisine.

Parsley, the most commonly used herb in Cajun-Creole cooking, is available most of the year and can be planted at home for ready access. More than just a garnish, parsley actually works to intensify the flavors in a dish and has a kind of "activating" aspect when added to a recipe. This trait is especially true when parsley is used in its fresh form instead of its dried one. As with my Sundried Tomato Hummus (Autumn), if the dish needs more flavor, simply combine additional fresh chopped parsley to bring out the natural citrus of the lemon or the tang of the sundried tomatoes.

Similarly, **rosemary**, my favorite woody herb, can be grown year-round without fear of its dying in "cold" winter days. Rosemary has a uniquely fragrant aspect that, while robust, complements everything from starchy potatoes in my Roasted Red Potatoes with Rosemary (Spring), to cool-weather squashes in Rosemary's Rosemary Pumpkin Soup (Autumn), or just as a simple herb rub for chicken or steak.

Basil and **thyme** represent the sweet aromatic herbs of this book that can make any dish just a little bit better. Basil occurs throughout my recipes as a primary ingredient instead of as a secondary spice. See my Watermelon Juice with Basil (Summer) or my Pea Pesto with Sundried Tomatoes (Spring) for an idea of how sweet basil brings life to a dish. I advocate the use of sweet basil specifically over lemon basil or holy basil because of its body and flavor. As for thyme, this woodier herb functions as a secondary spice that will enhance simple Stuffed Mushrooms (Spring) or Easy Roasted Garlic made specifically with thyme (Autumn). I

have lumped these two herbs together to emphasize their equal levels of importance: when keeping fresh primary spices on hand, always store and grow basil and when keeping secondary spices on hand, always store and grow thyme.

OLIVE OIL: Olive oils top my list of ingredients to have on hand as they are essential in the roasting, searing, cooking, and yes even *baking* of many recipes within this book. By themselves, virgin and extra-virgin olive oils—ones that contain no additives, chemicals, or solvents and come from the *first* pressing of the olive—add wonderful natural flavor to vegetables and meats without leaving behind greasy excess. In baking, regular olive oil (that is to say, oil that isn't of the virgin or extra-virgin variety) can be used instead of vegetable oil for adding healthy benefits to moist breads and cakes. As for extra-virgin and virgin olive oils, I reserve these more expensive varieties for dressings and garnishes, especially when dealing with infused varieties.

Throughout *The Fresh Table* I will suggest the use of infused olive oils, as they've a certain trick for adding instant flavor to a dish without actually including a second ingredient. Whether it's popping popcorn in spicy jalapeño olive oil or making pesto with part basil olive oil, the possibilities for cooking with infused olive oils are quite endless.

Consequently, as a chef, you become pretty attached (if not loyal) to certain companies and their products. I'll never forget the day my good friend Michael— whose recipe for Mac and Blue Cheese you can read in the Autumn section of this book—introduced me to infused olive oils and vinegars after a hot day on Magazine Street in New Orleans. We spent an hour tasting different variations, and I spent way too much money on some staples that I now find absolutely necessary in my own kitchen. Every cook has their secrets, and I feel strongly that the use of infused olive oils—with everything from exotic expensive goods like truffles to common herbs like basil or cayenne—are part of what make my homegrown recipes clearly delicious.

VINEGARS (I.E., BALSAMIC): Many chefs keep balsamic vinegar on hand, but rarely use it for more than the specific purpose of making a salad dressing. But, like infused olive oils, vinegars offer new ways to prepare the same old menu items. I've come to rely on infused vinegars when preparing homemade salad dressings, roasting certain vegetables, or just adding a drop or two to a glass of champagne. With the high-quality infused balsamics suggested in parts of this book, you can treat the vinegar as more of a *syrup* for baking and cooking. I always keep a bottle of my favorite cherry-infused balsamic vinegar on my home bar for adding color and flavor to cocktails. But for those readers new to the use of infused vinegars, I suggest selecting one infusion as your favorite that will carry you through the seasons. New Orleans-based company Vom Fass offers a free tasting room to all of its customers and will help you select the right variety for your kitchen. To see this and other companies' whole catalogues of options, visit the list of reliable online resources in the back of this book.

Useful Substitutions for Missing Equipment: For When You Just Can't Find That Kitchen Tool

TOOL		SUBSTITUTE
No Ravioli Press?	→	An Overturned Glass
No Grill Basket?	→	Grill Spears or Aluminum Foil
No Infused Olive Oil?	→	Regular Olive Oil plus the Ingredient of the Infusion
No Chicken Broth?	→	Vegetable or Beef Broth
No Boudin?	→	Any Good Sausage
No Tony's?	→	Salt + Cayenne
No Pie Crust?	→	Store-Bought Pie Crust Dough
No Pizza Dough?	→	Store-Bought Pizza Dough

Cooking Methods, Techniques, and Food Preservation: Introduction to Those Extra Homemade Steps in the Kitchen

To Make Your Own Chili Powder from Dried Chilies: Using a standard coffee grinder as suggested in my equipment list, de-stem and place chilies whole into your grinder. Cover and press down grind button until chilies are the desired powder-like consistency.

Don't have a coffee grinder? Finely chop dried chilies and transfer to a mortar and pestle with good texture. Crush chilies until dusty and powder-like.

To Make Pizza Dough: Follow the below recipe of warm water, active dry yeast, bread flour, salt, and sugar into the process of making a dough ball. This recipe can be used for any of the pizzas in this book and is improvised upon easily with the addition of fresh herbs, garlic, or other spices.

1½ cups warm water

2¼ teaspoons yeast (active dry variety)

3½ cups bread flour

2 tablespoons olive oil

2 teaspoons sugar

2 teaspoon salt

1 Add active yeast to warm water (preferably in a Kitchen-Aid mixing bowl) and rest until foamy or "activated" (about five minutes).

2 Add salt, sugar, and flour to yeast and water mixture, using dough hook on low speed. Continue mixing until a sticky dough forms.

3 Add 2 tablespoons olive oil to pizza dough and coat the dough ball fully. Allow dough to rest at room temperature for about an hour in a covered bowl. When dough has doubled in size, "punch" it down or use immediately. Dough can be refrigerated for up to a month and frozen for up to three months. Yields 2 pizza crusts.

To Make Pizza Sauce: Red sauces can be made from canned tomatoes, fresh tomatoes, or a combination of the two. Most often prepared with a variety of herbs—basil, rosemary, thyme, and/or parsley—homemade pizza sauce adds an outstanding gourmet element to dinnertime. The Red Sauce recipe and technique suggested here works for any of the pizza recipes in this book—Fig and Prosciutto Pizza (Summer), Boudin Pizza (Summer), and Pizza Florentine (Spring). Red Sauce may also be used to bed the Pumpkin-Encrusted Chicken Parmesan (Autumn) or to dress a simple plate of pasta.

½ onion, chopped fine

2 tablespoons olive oil

3 pounds vine-ripe tomatoes, chopped fine

3–4 cloves garlic, minced or pressed

½ cup basil, chopped fine

1 tablespoon rosemary, chopped fine

1 tablespoon thyme, chopped fine

salt and pepper, to taste

1 Add onions and olive oil to a nonstick skillet over medium heat and sauté until onions are golden. Add tomatoes, garlic, and herbs to skillet and bring to a light boil. Reduce heat to a low simmer and cook sauce covered until thickened (about 10–15 minutes). Season sauce with salt and pepper and taste. Continue to simmer until the sauce coats the back of a spoon and is the desired thickness. Makes 2½–3 cups sauce depending on amount of reduction and size of tomatoes.

Want to add a unique Cajun-Creole twist to your red sauce? Include the addition of paprika, chili powder, or Tony Chachere's Cajun seasoning for a more Creole flare. Season to taste with any combination of these three spices.

To Make Your Own Pasta Dough for Ravioli: Really one of the more advanced techniques in this cooking primer, making your own pasta dough demands extraordinary attention to the sticky-toughness of your dough ball, and the cautious use of rolling out and cooking with this dough. When making the below recipe, the best point to keep in mind will be to make sure not to reuse the dough if you don't have to. When preparing spaghetti, linguini, ravioli, or any pasta item at home, it is always best to make the pasta from the *first* pass of the dough. Just as overkneading biscuits or yeast bread will make the bread tough, so will the overkneading and second passing of pasta. Here, I suggest the use of handheld tools like a rolling pin, but a standard pasta machine works wonders with this recipe. For an example of how to use this specific pasta dough, see my Pumpkin Sage Ravioli recipe (Autumn), or use for my Crawfish Étouffée Ravioli (Summer).

3½ cups all-purpose flour

1 teaspoon olive oil

1 teaspoon salt

5 large eggs

1 In a standing mixer, attach the dough hook and combine flour, olive oil, salt, and eggs for three minutes until a dough ball forms. Cover with plastic wrap and rest for thirty minutes at room temperature.

2 Using a rolling pin and a well-floured surface, roll out dough as thinly as you possibly can. It's essential that when making ravioli, you do a single pass through with the pasta processing; otherwise the dough will be tough and so will the pasta. So, roll out the dough as thin as possible and cut based on the kind of pasta you are making (about 25–32 ounces pasta dough).

OPTION 1: If you are making spaghetti, angel hair, or linguini, a pizza cutter works great for cutting long thin strips with considerable control and ease. Cut thin strips from rolled-out pasta by tracing the side of a flat surface laid across your dough. Transfer strips to a wax paper surface (lying flat) until ready to cook in boiling water. Cook pasta in boiling salt water until *al dente* (firm, but cooked all the way through). Makes 1½–2 pounds pasta.

OPTION 2: If you are making ravioli, place teaspoon-size dollops of choice filling evenly throughout the pasta sheet. I use my ravioli press as a stencil by making indentations into the bottom half of the dough and then filling them with filling. This way, I have a marker for how many pieces I will be making and never run out of dough. Carefully fold half of the dough on top of itself and press down the edges making a note of where each filling dollop is placed. Using a single ravioli press (or overturned glass), punch out the individual squares (or circles) for each piece. Transfer raviolis to a plate lined with parchment paper and repeat until all of the dough has been used. Cook raviolis in boiling salt water until *al dente.* Makes 3–4 dozen raviolis based on size of ravioli press.

To Make Your Own Pie Crust: Homemade pie crust tastes amazing whether you use a lard- or butter-based recipe. In my kitchen, I always opt for the butter recipe as it can be used for savory dishes like Crawfish Potpies (Winter) and Individual Beef Wellingtons (Winter) or sweet ones such as any fruit pie and rustic *galette*. If using the butter recipe here, expect a golden, flaky, melt-in-your mouth crust that wows. However, substitute half of the butter with lard for an even *flakier* crust that many home cooks love.

2½ cups flour, more for dusting

2 sticks of unsalted butter, cut into
1-inch cubes and frozen

1 teaspoon kosher salt

2 teaspoons sugar

3–5 tablespoons ice water

1   Begin by freezing the butter. Place 2 sticks unsalted butter cut into 1-inch cubes into freezer and rest for at least 15 minutes, but preferably an hour. The longer the better, as cold butter is key to a perfect crust.

2   Add flour, salt, and sugar to a food processor. Pulse to combine.

3   When butter is adequately frozen remove the 1-inch cubes and roughly chop (I suggest quartering the 1-inch cubes). Add to food processor and pulse until mixture resembles coarse meal.

4   Slowly add ice water to processor until a ball forms. You'll know it's done because a ball will quite literally form in the processor. Stop adding water immediately once your dough ball comes together.

5   Flour a surface and add dough ball to surface. Divide in half and create two circular discs. Now, you can either cover the dough balls in plastic wrap and refrigerate or freeze for future use or you can roll them out for immediate use. When cooking, crust will be done when golden brown and flaky. Makes 2 pie crusts.

To Roast Your Own Red Peppers: Roasted red peppers are so easily available at any major grocery store that readers may find it humorous I include their preparation here. However, like any dish that's made with love and homemade care, home-roasted red peppers have a flavor that makes store-bought ones taste like nothing at all. The difference between the two lies in the robust sweet flavors of fresh red peppers whereas canned or jarred roasted peppers have an element of unexciting age.

Roast your own red peppers for my Summer Gazpacho with Avocado and Cucumber or top on a pizza with Boudin.

4 red peppers, whole and washed

kosher salt, for sprinkling

2–3 tablespoons extra virgin olive oil

1   Roast peppers whole over an open flame until the skin is completely charred. You can do this step with a charcoal grill, flame from one of your gas stove's burners, or by simply blistering the fruit under a high broiler until the skin is black (rotating halfway through to blister whole fruit). Depending on cooking technique, this step could take anywhere from 10 to 20 minutes.

2   Transfer roasted peppers to a chopping board and rest until room temperature. Peel blistered skins off and discard with the help of cold water. Using a chef's or paring knife, lop off tops of red peppers, remove seeds, halve, and cut into thin slices (making sure to reserve the red fruit by the stem as it's still good). Place roasted peppers in a glass jar with 3 tablespoons olive oil and a heavy pinch of kosher salt. Cover with lid and shake. Refrigerate fruit over night so that it may set and keep for up to two weeks in the refrigerator.

To Prevent Chocolate from Separating: When the melting of chocolate is mentioned—for my Candied Pears (Autumn), Orangettes (Winter), or any other melting step listed in this book—I often suggest the use of a standard kitchen thermometer. Chocolate can be a finicky ingredient and is prone to separating and becoming greasy if it gets too hot. To prevent the disastrous results of overheating your chocolate, keep thermometer in chocolate when melting on the stovetop with a little bit of cream and do not allow the temperature to rise above 115F.

To Roll an Egg Roll: Used best for my Avocado Egg Rolls with Honey Cilantro Asian Dipping Sauce (Summer). You will need to rely on this tip only once. Think of rolling an egg roll like rolling a cigarette. Although I don't smoke, the concept makes perfect sense: you do *not* want to overfill your paper (here, the egg roll sheet), and you must make sure to safely tuck in the sides of your paper before rolling it longways. Here's how the process should go:

1 Fill egg roll sheet with desired amount of avocado, making sure not to overstuff. Taking the two short ends of the sheet (what would representatively be the tips of a cigarette), fold the ends inward about ½ to 1 inch.

2 Now, rolling long-ways, push the top of the avocado sheet into its filling mixture and roll away from you until you have a tube-like egg roll. This step may take some practice, but is much easier than it sounds.

Always, make sure to wet the edges of your egg roll paper before rolling so that the paper will stick to itself. I suggest the use of a beaten egg or egg yolk here.

To Cook a Steak by Levels of Doneness: Perhaps one of the most useful tips in this section, checking the doneness of a steak is much simpler than cutting open and reading whether or not it has a pink line. When I was working in a kitchen as a teenager, our chef taught me the oldest trick for reading meat on the grill: the hand (or "finger") doneness test. I always advise this technique to my friends and fellow foodies. Once you've tried it a few times, you'll be surprised just how easy the trick is to remember and just how intuitive the process becomes. Many readers may already be familiar with this method, but for those of you new to the technique, here's what to do.

HAND (OR "FINGER") DONENESS TEST:

RAW: Open the palm of your nonprimary hand and relax. Using the forefinger of your primary hand, press into the other hand's flesh between your wrist and thumb (the fleshy mound at the base of your thumb). Here, the flesh will be easy to press and represents what raw meat feels like—impressionable and easy to add force to.

MEDIUM-RARE: This is tougher in sensation than the relaxed palm, or "raw" finger, test. You can see if a steak is medium-rare by pressing it as you do when touching your middle finger to the tip of your thumb. The same mound at the base of your thumb will be impressionable, but a little harder to add force to. This tougher sensation indicates a more cooked steak at medium-rare.

MEDIUM: Bring the tip of your thumb to the tip of your ring finger and add pressure to the mound at the base of your thumb as before. The mound should be tougher, but still impressionable. This balance between force and resistance is what medium-cooked meat feels like.

WELL-DONE: Last, using your shortest digit (pinky finger), bring the tip of your thumb to the tip of your pinky. The mound beneath your thumb should feel quite firm and give very little if at all to pressure.

To Remove Pomegranate Seeds: Cut pomegranate in half and lightly pull seeds away from white tissue siding. I like to "massage" the seeds out instead of spooning or pulling them from the rind. This way, you rarely crush the berries and make use of the entire pomegranate. Having trouble with removing seeds from a halved pomegranate? Quarter the fruit and start there. Increased surface area of the exposed seeds (when quartered) will make massaging out stubborn fruit much easier.

To Cut an Avocado or Mango: One of the most useful tips in this section, cutting an avocado or mango is really quite simple, so long as you follow my "hedgehog" technique. Both avocado meat and mango fruit have thick pits that affect the way in which they can be prepared. Unlike an avocado, which can be pitted quite easily, a mango requires that you sense the location of its hairy pit (the seed) and cut the flesh away from there. For the avocado, you'll need to remove the seed from the green meat, but carefully.

AVOCADO: Using a paring knife, slice down the center of a ripe avocado making note of where the tip of the knife meets the seed. Cut all the way around the avocado, set down knife, and with one half of the avocado in each hand, *pull* the fruit apart. A ripe avocado will give easily and the pit should remain stuck to one of its sides. Lay pit side of avocado face-up and being very careful to press the tip of your paring knife into the pit, press and twist until the seed comes out. Again, the riper the avocado, the easier this step will be. Discard seed and cut like a hedgehog: tracing the outer ridges of where the green meat comes up to the shell, cut all the way around. Then, cut several vertical strips from the tip of the avocado to its bottom and repeat this step with horizontal incisions. Lay down knife and, pinching the dark green shell in both hands, flex the skin backwards until the squared meat *pops up* like a hedgehog. From here, you can cut the fruit from the skin or simply pull it off.

MANGO: As with an avocado, you want to use a sharp paring knife for this fruit. Stand mango straight up and cut all the way down on both sides removing the "cheeks" of the fruit. Lay cheeks to the side and carve off excess ripe fruit from the seed. Since the seed is the same color as the fleshy fruit, it'll be hard to gauge exactly where all of the excess fruit may be carved. A good rule of thumb is to carve as close to the hairy pit as possible in a 360-degree fashion so that all of the skinned fruit has now been removed from the pit. To remove fruit from mango skin, follow the hedgehog technique above in the avocado section. For scrap pieces of fruit, simply use your paring knife to peel skin away from the mango's yellow meat.

To Make Almond Meal: This tip takes very little time with the help of a standard coffee grinder and arises several times throughout the course of this book either with the addition of sugar to almonds or flour to almonds. Generally speaking, "almond meal" simply refers to the process of combining fresh almonds with all-purpose flour, cake flour, or powdered sugar to create a mixture that is part flour, sugar, and almonds, or "almond meal." You will need this technique for my almond crust in the Glazed Tarte aux Baies (Spring) and any cheesecake crust (Summer) that calls for almond meal. Here's how:

2 tablespoons confectioner's sugar

1 cup sliced almonds

1 Pulse 2 tablespoons confectioner's sugar with sliced almonds in a coffee grinder. Grind until a fine powder develops. Add almond meal to a dish with all-purpose flour or any other flour necessary for an almond-infused crust. Makes ½ cup.

To Infuse Olive Oils: Since many home chefs may not have the same olive oil infusions I suggest in this book, you may easily get around this missing ingredient by making your own infusions at home with herbs, fruits, rinds, and nuts. Most commonly, I refer to basil-infused olive oil, cayenne-infused olive oil, or walnut-infused olive oil. See the recipe below for a quick and easy infusion using basil, but substitute any infusion ingredient in this book for the same results.

4 cups extra virgin olive oil

2 cups packed and chopped basil

1 Clean a glass jar that will hold 6 cups of infused olive oil and add four cups olive oil to it.

2 Chop basil thinly and add to olive oil.

3 Stir to integrate and seal jar tightly. Refrigerate immediately and discard after one week both to ensure freshness and prevent the growth of microbes. Makes 4 cups basil-infused olive oil.

spring

MARCH–MAY

Springtime in Louisiana is a fabulous season to begin dabbling in local seasonal cooking. Succeeding winter's shallots, root vegetables, and rich citrus season of oranges and lemons, springtime produce embraces past popular crops with newly abundant selections. Strawberries, English peas, artichokes, and spinach mark some of the most marketed options in Louisiana during the months of March–May while lemons and other varieties of citrus are still readily available. In this section, herbs such as mint, rosemary, and lavender are incorporated into a variety of sweet and savory dishes while chicken, Boudin, oysters, tuna, and shrimp find their ways into these dishes as well.

Mango Salsa

Petite Crab Cakes with Cajun Dipping Sauce

Pea Pesto Crostini with Red Spring Onions,
   Shaved Parmesan, and Toasted Pine Nuts
   or Sundried Tomatoes

Spinach Artichoke Dip with Spicy Cayenne

Strawberry Brie Bruschetta

Peeled Zucchini and Asparagus Salad with Spicy Wasabi

Antipasti Avocado Asparagus Salad

Velvety Asparagus Soup

Pizza Florentine

Seared Ahi Tuna

Bowtie Spinach Pesto Pasta with Wild Mushrooms

Beer Can Chicken

Grilled Oysters with Bacon and Butter

Artichokes with Red Pepper Aioli

Stuffed Mushrooms

Glazed Honey Shrimp Skewers

Green Beans with Almonds

Roasted Red Potatoes with Rosemary

Lemon Cake with Lemon Buttercream Icing

Strawberry Pavlova with Chocolate

Glazed Tarte aux Baies (French Berry Tart)

Strawberry Cake with Strawberry Buttercream Frosting

Fruit Salad Bake with Curry

Savory Crêpes Boudin

Bananas Foster Croissant French Toast

Absinthe (a New Orleans tradition)

Southern Mint Julep

Lemon Lavender Muffins

APPETIZERS

Mango Salsa

LIKE MOST PEOPLE, I've come to love that there are as many ways to make salsa as there are vegetables and fruits to imagine it—traditional tomato salsa, fruity salsa with cantaloupes, tomatillo salsa, or veggie salsas with crisp cucumbers and tangy limes.

Although it's not yet summer, springtime in Baton Rouge evokes the early heat of summer days, and I'm just crazy for early spring appetizers that cool my body and feed my appetite. My easy and sweet take on mango salsa makes for a refreshing answer for any hot and hungry spring day.

The beauty of this fruity salsa variation lies, partly, in the very few ingredients one requires to make it—fresh tomatoes and ripe mangoes tossed in lime juice and cilantro. Season to taste with salt and pepper, and you have a new twist on an everyday classic. Dip into this salsa with your favorite tortilla chips or just eat it with a spoon. After all, the tradition of salsa lies in its ability to be modified.

Mango salsa can be adapted in a number of ways. For a variation that involves a satisfying veggie crunch, add cucumbers or several tablespoons of minced onion.

3 mangos (Ataulfo mango used here, but Kent mangos are also delicious), cubed "hedgehog" style

2 roma tomatoes, seeded and diced

2 limes, juiced

1 large handful cilantro, chopped fine

salt and pepper, to taste

1   Cut mango using the hedgehog technique listed in the how-to section of the Introduction and add to a bowl. Chop roma tomatoes, remove seeds, and add to combine. Squeeze fresh lime juice over mixture and toss with salt, pepper, and a handful of finely chopped cilantro. Makes 4 servings.

Petite Crab Cakes with Cajun Dipping Sauce

AMONG THE MANY seafood options Gulf Coast fishermen make readily available to Louisiana residents, fresh crab meat constitutes one of my all-time favorites. Underneath the hard shells lies soft, delicately textured meat that works beautifully in dips, stuffings, and, my favorite, crab cakes. Even northern restaurants prize our unique crabs, with many Louisiana crustaceans finding themselves in Maryland restaurants—our excess crab products going not to local bellies, but often to out-of-state gastronomes.

Despite my love of all things Gulf Coast seafood, the Louisiana crab industry has taken a bit of a beating in recent years. Between Hurricane Katrina and the BP Oil Spill, crab culture here has undergone some bizarre twists with stories of whole fishing coastal towns being eradicated.

As chefs, we have a certain duty to keep Gulf seafood industries going, so eat up with these simple Petite Crab Cakes with Cajun Dipping Sauce. Although many people in Louisiana eat crab cakes as an entrée, I suggest wowing your guests immediately with an appetizer that is as decadent as the real meal itself. You'll be indulging in a coastal favorite and perhaps even doing a little something for the coast.

The art to a really great crab cake is getting the cakes to stick together. In the early days of my blog, I found this task so difficult that I swore crab cakes could only be baked in the oven. It turns out that with enough culinary "glue"—here, butter crackers and an egg—the well-formed stovetop variation of this appetizer is deliciously probable.

CRAB CAKES

1 pound real crab meat

⅓ cup crushed butter crackers such as Ritz

2 green onions, chopped fine

¼ of a red bell pepper, chopped fine

¼ of a green bell pepper, chopped fine

1 Prep ingredients for crab cakes: Chop bell peppers, parsley, and green onions. Measure out spices.

2 Mix together ingredients: Crab meat, crackers, onions, peppers, egg, Worcestershire sauce, mayonnaise, lemon juice, Grey Poupon, and spices—salt, pepper, paprika, parsley, and thyme.

1 teaspoon coarse salt

1 large egg

2 teaspoons Worcestershire sauce

1 teaspoon paprika

1 teaspoon freshly ground black pepper

2 tablespoons mayonnaise (spicy mayonnaise if you have it)

¼ cup parsley, chopped fine

½ lemon, squeezed: reserve half of the juice for dipping sauce recipe

2 tablespoons spicy or Dijon-style mustard such as Grey Poupon

½ teaspoon fresh or ground thyme

oil for frying, such as peanut or regular vegetable oil, which works well too

SAUCE

1½ cups mayonnaise

1 tablespoon tomato paste

2 tablespoons spicy or Dijon-style mustard such as Grey Poupon

½ tablespoon thyme

1 tablespoon parsley, chopped fine

½–1 tablespoon lemon juice, freshly squeezed from above

1–2 garlic cloves, pressed or minced

1 teaspoon Worcestershire sauce

1–2 teaspoons cayenne, to taste

salt and pepper, to taste

3   Shape crab cake mixture into small patties less than half the size of a regular full-bodied crab cake. Cakes half the size of your palm will be just the right size.

4   In a large skillet, warm oil to medium-high and place crab cakes evenly apart in pan. Try not to overcrowd your pan, as flipping the cakes will be very difficult and the cooking times will be much longer.

5   Fry cakes on both sides until browned. Based on cooking heat and temperature, this step could take as little as 3–4 minutes or as much as 5–6 for each side. Carefully flip cakes to prevent them from falling apart. Plate and serve warm with Cajun Dipping Sauce. Makes 6 cakes.

6   Prepare Cajun Dipping Sauce: Add all ingredients to a food processor and pulse until creamy. Taste and adjust flavors as necessary—you may wish to add more salt, pepper, or cayenne.

7   Serve with Petite Crab Cakes and refrigerate any leftovers. Sauce keeps for up to a month.

If keeping cakes whole is giving you difficulty, press a fork down into the top of the cake while you flip it with your spatula. This sandwiching effect helps to prevent any gravitational crumbling.

Pea Pesto Crostini with Red Spring Onions, Shaved Parmesan, and Toasted Pine Nuts or Sundried Tomatoes

PESTO

1 cup garden or sweet peas, cooked fresh or frozen

1 cup fresh sweet basil, chopped fine

½ cup fresh Parmesan cheese, shredded (*not* canned Parmesan)

1 teaspoon kosher salt, plus more to taste

½ teaspoon ground black pepper, plus more for seasoning

⅓ cup basil olive oil, such as the one in this book or one from Vom Fass New Orleans, or regular olive oil

3 cloves garlic, minced or pressed

¼ cup pistachios, chopped

CROSTINI TOPPERS

1 Ciabatta bread loaf, Seeduction Bread (Whole Foods), or any other baguette alternative

baby spring red onions, halved right where the red bulb meets the green stalk

sundried tomatoes packed without oil; can use the oil-packed ones if you must

salt and pepper, for dusting

olive oil, for dressing

¼ cup pine nuts, toasted in 1 tablespoon olive oil

PEA PESTO IS ONE of those dishes that I've had many dinner guests jump back in surprise over the contents. The idea of combining peas with a traditional basil pesto seems like the stuff of little kiddy dinners—"Eat your peas, honey!"—but really represents one of the most sweetly flavored variations of pesto I've ever had. Introduced to me by one Dr. Robert Hamm, LSU professor of Shakespeare and Renaissance literature and a fantastic domestic gourmand, this pea pesto is one that will impress any dinner guest.

Serve pesto as a spread on toasted hardy bread as suggested here, or dress over pasta as a sauce as suggested with my Bowtie Pasta and Wild Mushrooms in the entrée section for spring.

I suggest using the Ciabatta Bread recipe from the Winter section for Breakfast, but you can easily substitute a whole-wheat bread such as Whole Foods' Seeduction Bread or a warm French baguette. Since many gardens in Louisiana yield the sweetest of spring and summer peas, feel free to substitute your own garden's contents over more readily available frozen sweet peas.

1   Thaw and cook sweet peas if using the frozen variation. If using the garden fresh variety, cook fresh peas in hot water and sit for about 5 minutes removed from heat. Drain peas.

2   Add peas, Parmesan, basil, garlic, salt, pepper, olive oil, and pistachios to food processor and pulse to combine until creamy. Don't worry about overpulsing this mixture, as a little bit of texture from the sweet peas is always a fabulous component.

3   Spread pesto mixture on bread choice and top with halved spring red onion bulbs and pine nuts or sundried tomatoes. Dust both options in salt and pepper and a few drops of olive oil for each crostini. Makes 12–15 crostini.

Spinach Artichoke Dip with Spicy Cayenne

SPINACH WILL ALWAYS be one of my favorite vegetables—its soft but slightly crisp leafy greens go great with just about anything: dressed in balsamic vinegar, tossed with Gorgonzola cheese, or yes, even slowly roasted with cream cheese, Parmesan, and artichoke hearts. My variation for this popular dip is a step up from a regular spinach artichoke dip recipe we see at most restaurants with attention to spicy peppers that grow fresh in Louisiana gardens starting in the spring months. For a traditional variation (that isn't Louisiana spicy), skip the steps involving cayenne and paprika.

For chefs new to the flavors of Louisiana, the addition of Tony Chachere's Cajun Seasoning is an easy way to introduce Cajun spices into a simple appetizer or dip. Its blend of salt and cayenne make for a salty and spicy ingredient with which it's easy to measure and experiment.

Looking for a new way to enjoy fresh Spinach Artichoke Dip with Spicy Cayenne any season? For spinach substitute roasted winter broccoli, spring asparagus, or even summer zucchini for a dip that is equally as hardy and delicious.

10 ounces frozen spinach, thawed and drained (about 1½ cups)

1 (8-ounce) package regular cream cheese, not low fat, softened

1 cup freshly grated Parmesan, plus more for topping

⅓ cup sour cream, regular

⅓ cup mayonnaise

1 (15.5-ounce) can artichoke hearts, drained

4 cloves garlic, pressed or minced

2 teaspoons cayenne, or substitute 1 spicy pepper from spring garden

paprika, for dusting

Tony Chachere's and pepper, to taste

1   Preheat oven to 375F. Mix together spinach, cream cheese, Parmesan, sour cream, mayonnaise, artichoke hearts, garlic, and spices. Taste and adjust with any necessary Tony Chachere's or pepper. Spread mixture into an ovenproof casserole dish, sprinkle with Parmesan and paprika (and cayenne, if you're feeling extra dangerous), and bake until the top of the mixture is golden brown, about 25–30 minutes.

2   Serve with toasted baguette or Ciabatta from the Winter Breakfast section, crackers, or any other favorite dipping choice. Serves 10–12 people.

Strawberry Brie Bruschetta

WHEN I WAS a little girl, my mother used to take my sister and me berry picking. We'd fill whole baskets with wild strawberries, go home, and eat them out of bowls while watching movies. If we had been "real good," she'd treat us to toasted bread with butter, jam, and fresh strawberry slices.

This bruschetta offers a somewhat grown-up variation of one of my favorite childhood recipes complete with Brie and crusty bread.

I suggest toasting your baguette here, but the bruschetta is equally lovely when placed on nontoasted baguette and warmed under the broiler.

1 pint strawberries, stemmed and washed

2 heaping tablespoons sugar

1 teaspoon almond extract

1 Brie wheel, rind removed

1 baguette or other crusty bread, sliced

3–4 tablespoons olive oil

½ cup almonds, whole or sliced

1 Prepare ingredients: Wash and stem strawberries and remove rind from Brie wheel. Cut Brie and strawberries into slices and add to a bowl with almond extract and sugar. Mix strawberries to combine and allow them to rest for at least 30 minutes so that they might macerate. At 30 minutes, press down strawberries with a fork, gently, and stir to coat fruit in natural juices.

2 In a nonstick skillet, warm enough olive oil to cover the bottom of the pan thinly (most likely 1–2 tablespoons, but you will need to continue adding more as you progressively toast more baguette slices). Add slices of baguette and toast until golden brown and flip to toast other side. Plate bread for dressing.

3 Dress bread with slices of Brie and top with strawberries and almonds. Makes 10–12 servings.

Peeled Zucchini and Asparagus Salad
with Spicy Wasabi

I'M FINDING THAT few of my friends ever eat their vegetables raw. Many perceive raw, uncooked produce as the stuff of salads, the stuff of calorie-inhibiting, bathing-suit-season goals. Raw vegetables are some unprocessed monster looking to make us keenly aware of all the carbs and sugars we're depriving ourselves of while we dream of skinnier days.

In a single phrase, uncooked vegetables often find themselves clumped into the category of "diet" food.

But are they really diet food? Aren't carrot sticks wonderful? Isn't a fresh tomato with salt better than a cooked one? And what about sweet red bell peppers? I'll eat those raw over mushy cooked versions any day.

To combat the American cook-everything-or-try-to-fry-it way, I suggest taking baby steps this Spring—my simple but elegant Zucchini and Asparagus Salad with Spicy Wasabi is as beautiful as it is fresh, and noticeably healthy. Peel several washed asparagus spears and one zucchini into shreds, toss with a light vinaigrette of olive oil and lemon juice, season with salt and pepper, and garnish with spicy wasabi. It has perhaps more flavor than any cooked variation of spicy Asian vegetables I've ever seen. But I must say, the low-calorie bathing-suit benefits are just a lucky perk.

1 zucchini, stems removed, washed, and peeled into thin slivers

3–4 asparagus spears, washed and thinly peeled

salt and pepper, to taste

1–2 tablespoons olive oil

1–2 tablespoons lemon juice

Wasabi Horseradish Cream Sauce, or any like spicy Asian sauce, for garnishing

1 Wash zucchini and asparagus and remove stems. Using a standard peeler, peel vegetables into a large bowl (skins included).

2 Toss vegetable slices in olive oil, lemon juice, and salt and pepper. Taste and adjust spices accordingly.

3 Plate zucchini and asparagus salad in a stacked spiral and serve with Wasabi Horseradish Cream Sauce as a side and dip. Makes 4 servings.

If you find that your dinner companions are not fans of the Asian-spin with spicy wasabi, serve this salad without the wasabi in just a simple olive oil and lemon juice vinaigrette.

Antipasti Avocado Asparagus Salad

ONE OF MY favorite springtime vegetables, asparagus, tastes just as wonderful raw as with the use of raw zucchini in my Peeled Zucchini and Asparagus Salad with Spicy Wasabi. Here, I continue my love affair with clean spring produce by combining it with the creamy texture of ripe avocados for an impressive start to any meal. Serve with a simple dressing of olive oil and lemon juice for a fresh addition.

1 cup spinach, or arugula

¼ cup cherry tomatoes, halved

small handful dried cranberries

less than ¼ cup cucumbers, peeled and halved

½ avocado, cut into strips

¼ cup red bell pepper, cut into strips (can substitute roasted red peppers—see recipe in "Cooking Methods, Techniques, and Food Preservation")

handful of asparagus spears, de-stemmed, lightly peeled

2 tablespoons olive oil

½ lemon, juiced

cheese of choice: I sprinkled my salad with goat cheese, but Gorgonzola, blue, or another soft cheese works great here too

¼ cup toasted pecans

1   Prepare ingredients: Wash produce and halve/peel/slice accordingly. Set aside.

2   In a small saucepan, warm olive oil. Add asparagus spears and sauté for 3–5 minutes until tender, but still crispy on medium heat.

3   Plate salad with spinach, tomatoes, cranberries, cucumbers, red bell pepper, pecans, top with fresh avocado strips and asparagus spears, and sprinkle with soft cheese. Serve salad with a light vinaigrette made from 1 tablespoon olive oil and ½ of a lemon, juiced. Makes 1 serving.

SOUPS

Velvety Asparagus Soup

NOTHING REALLY SAYS "I love you" like a homemade bowl of soup. Whether you're making it for a sick child, a sick boyfriend or girlfriend, or under the complete and total promise that it will keep someone you love warm in the winter months while you're away, soup is the ultimate homemade care package steaming with affection.

Before leaving for a much-needed trip to New England one Christmas holiday, I wanted to show a close friend that I cared. So, I made him soup. And, I showed him how to make it too.

People are often fixated on the speed at which I cook in my kitchen. If recipe making were a timed sport, I'd win the gold metal with every dish. But making soup shouldn't be a rushed process. It's a slow and simmering procedure based on the addition of ingredients and the waiting for the introduction of each ingredient.

Teaching someone to cook is exactly this way. For someone who has never really prepared their own food, or even made soup before, the mystery of making soup from raw ingredients is about as complicated as one of those cars that are really cakes on Food Network. So, one must pace one's self when teaching a loved one how to cook soup, especially when that loved one gave you the recipe book itself.

In a nutshell, my version of this asparagus velouté soup combines a simple roux with steaming vegetable broth, pureed, blanched asparagus, and thickening agents of cream and egg yolks with salt and pepper to taste. It's so perfect in its final stage, so fully embodied in flavor that as the soup becomes thicker and thicker, there can be no doubt that you care.

Inspired by a classic asparagus soup in the Larousse Gastronomique cookbook, vegetables section, my version infuses a classic French recipe with the addition of chili powder.

8 tablespoons salted butter (3 tablespoons for roux and 5 tablespoons for broth)

5 tablespoons flour

3½ cups chicken broth

1 bunch asparagus (about 14 ounces), woody ends trimmed and blanched

3 egg yolks, beaten

8 tablespoons heavy cream

2 teaspoons chili powder

To Garnish (optional):

reserved asparagus tips

1 tablespoon parsley, chopped

¼ cup croutons

1   Begin by preparing a white roux: Whisk together butter and flour in a large soup pot. Add chicken broth to roux and continue whisking to combine.

2   Wash asparagus and remove woody ends by snapping off oversized, rough ends. Cut asparagus into thirds. Bring a small pot of water to a boil and add asparagus. Boil for 5 minutes. Add butter and simmer for 10 minutes. Drain asparagus and set aside.

3   Blend asparagus in a food processor or blender into a puree. Add pureed asparagus to chicken broth and mix to combine. Remove soup from heat and thicken with three beaten egg yolks. Add seven tablespoons of cream (can add less to taste) and reheat, but *do not boil.* Serve soup immediately and garnish with asparagus tips, chopped parsley, and croutons. Makes 6 servings.

ENTRÉES

Pizza Florentine

WHEN LIVING IN France, my friend Lauren had the strangest pizza with some of her friends—a hearty pizza pie with an egg cracked in the middle. She said the egg was cooked, but just enough so that you could pierce the yolk with a fork and spread it all over the cheesy topping so that the yolk-y flavor covered a little bit of every slice.

Folks, I would like to introduce you to my new friend Pizza Florentine. Any friend of Lauren's is certainly a friend of mine.

Legend has it that Pizza Florentine was invented as a breakfast pizza in Italy, but is often eaten today as an unadorned single-course meal. With the warming of spring and the abundance of local fresh eggs, this Italian classic deserves a new Louisiana twist! To make your pizza truly Louisiana, check into the number of organic egg grocers in the back of this book.

However you eat it—for breakfast, lunch, or dinner—Pizza Florentine with locally laid eggs (especially organic) combine some of my personal favorite earthy Italian spices with warm, gooey, melted cheese, rich red tomato sauce, and a hearty crust. It's no wonder an egg goes so well with these other flavors! It's breakfast AND pizza.

1 serving pizza dough (see recipe in "Cooking Methods, Techniques, and Food Preservation")

1 tablespoon olive oil

1–2 cups red sauce (tomato—either homemade or from the supermarket), to taste

salt and pepper, to taste

Italian herbs, to taste (I suggest thyme, rosemary, and parsley)

2 cups spinach

1½ cups mozzarella cheese, cubed

4 eggs, fresh

1   Preheat oven to 375F. On a clean, well-floured surface, roll out pre-made pizza dough into a circular round. Transfer to a pizza stone that has been sprinkled with corn meal.

2   Lightly drizzle olive oil on dough and brush to coat. Using a fork, evenly pierce the dough all over.

3   Dress pizza: Spread red tomato sauce on pizza and season with salt, pepper, and Italian herbs such as thyme, rosemary, and parsley. Top pizza with spinach, mozzarella, and the last of your seasonings (again with salt, pepper, and Italian herbs).

4 Bake pizza for 20–25 minutes or until pizza is almost done—the crust should be close to golden-brown at the edges and the mozzarella should also be starting to brown—but the pizza should not be completely browned or cooked through. Remove pizza from oven and carefully crack eggs in the center. Return pizza to oven and cook for an additional 8–10 minutes. You want to remove the pizza when the eggs are "done" where the whites are cooked, but the yolk is still warm and sauce-like.

5 Remove pizza from oven and allow to rest for 5 minutes. Cut into slices using a pizza cutter, or a Mezzaluna, and serve. Makes 4 servings (one pizza; double recipe for two).

Seared Ahi Tuna

A SIMPLE SEARED tuna makes a great base for any spring meal. Rub with subtle Asian spices, sear, and serve on a classic Louisiana remoulade salad to liven things up or plate with pea pesto to embrace two great ingredients the season has to offer. The light juicy meat beds nicely with a complex flavor for any fish-loving dinner guest.

Although I prefer ahi tuna to be cooked medium (with some pink in the middle) instead of medium-rare, ahi tuna tastes great so long as it's not well done. For the cooking method suggested here, sear the fish according to your personal preference, but be wary of overcooking.

1 teaspoon lime or lemon juice

1 green onion, thinly sliced plus extra for sprinkling on final dish

1 clove garlic, minced or pressed

1 tablespoon ginger

2 tablespoons soy sauce

2 tablespoons dark sesame, or peanut, oil

2 (6- or 8-ounce) ahi yellow fin tuna steaks

1   Begin by preparing the ahi tuna marinade: Mix citrus juice, green onion, garlic, ginger, soy sauce, and sesame or peanut oil in a bowl. Whisk to combine. Add tuna to mixture and coat thoroughly. Marinate fish for at least an hour, but can be refrigerated overnight.

2   Heat a nonstick skillet on medium-high heat for searing. When the pan is thoroughly hot, remove tuna steaks from marinade and sear for 1–4 minutes on each side: 1 minute on each side will yield an extremely rare steak, but 3–5 minutes will yield a more medium-to-well done (but still pink) tuna steak.

3   Remove from pan and cut into quarter-inch slices.

4   Plate and serve with Pea Pesto (recipe in the appetizers section of this season), and sprinkled green onions and/or cilantro. Makes 4 servings.

Bowtie Spinach Pesto Pasta with Wild Mushrooms

I'LL BE THE FIRST to admit that warm pasta may not be the perfect dinner item for my pre-bathing-suit-season skinny jeans. But this Bowtie Spinach Pesto Pasta with Wild Mushrooms is totally worth it . . . tumescent stomachs and all. The process is simple with its fresh green ingredients and it may have you forgetting your skinny jeans.

Just as peas make for a wonderful addition to any basic pesto recipe, so do fresh spinach leaves. When making this recipe, I always use half a bag of spinach for the pesto—about two cups packed—and the other half for a starter salad.

PESTO

2 cups fresh spinach, packed

1 cup fresh sweet basil, chopped fine

½ cup fresh Parmesan cheese, shredded (*not* canned Parmesan)

1 teaspoon kosher salt, plus more to taste

½ teaspoon ground black pepper, plus more for seasoning

⅓ cup basil olive oil, such as the one from Vom Fass New Orleans, or regular olive oil

3 garlic cloves, minced or pressed

¼ cup pistachios, chopped

PASTA

1 (12-ounce) box pasta, such as bowtie ("farfalle")

2 cups wild mushrooms

2 tablespoons walnut olive oil such as the kind from Fioré, or regular olive oil

1 Prepare the pesto: Pulse together fresh spinach with the sweet basil, olive oil, Parmesan, and roasted pistachios for an even greener take on a regular Italian sauce. Follow the same instructions available in the spring appetizers section.

2 Reserve pesto for tossing with pasta.

3 Prepare the pasta: Bring a large pot of salted water to a boil. In order for your pasta to have flavor, the best rule of thumb is to do exactly what the Italians do: pasta water should taste like "sea water." In many ways, I find this advice to be dangerous as it is possible to oversalt your cooking water. But, the point is well taken: don't be afraid to add *more than a little* salt to your cooking water.

4 Add pasta to boiling water and cook uncovered, stirring occasionally until *al dente* (firm to the palette, but done). Drain pasta and return to pot.

5 While pasta is cooking, roast mushrooms in olive oil until tender. Turn off heat.

6 Toss bowtie pasta in spinach pesto and roasted mushrooms and serve. Makes 8–10 servings.

It is unnecessary to wash fungi for cooking.

Beer Can Chicken

I AM ALWAYS looking for an easy, flavorful technique when preparing chicken. Often, I rely on tenderizers and broths during cooking, but I have become a huge fan of this locally popular variation—chicken self-steamed with a half-filled beer can.

This recipe is incredibly simple and the toughest part may just be picking the beer with which you wish to roast your chicken. Like most Louisianans, I find that Abita is one of my favorite beers, and the company announced that in 2012 it will begin producing Abita Amber, Purple Haze, and Jockamo IPA in a can. However, any canned beer will do the trick for this technique, but Abita is just so Louisiana.

As you pull out your grills this spring, try an easy chicken dish that gets its moisture from a steaming beer can. Perhaps it will be your new favorite too.

1 small (3–4 pound) chicken

seasonings to taste: salt, pepper, olive oil, and herbs (I prefer thyme and sage)

1 can of beer, half full

1   Rinse chicken, pat dry, and rub down in seasonings and oil. Using a half full beer can, lower the chicken onto the can as a stand.

2   For the grill: Fire up grill to nice and hot and place chicken over center of heat with the can and legs acting as a sort of three-legged tripod. Cover chicken, making sure not to open the grill until at least 45 minutes have passed. Check temperature of chicken with a meat thermometer: chicken should read 165F in the fleshiest part of its thigh to be done. Refresh coals if chicken isn't done and cook for an additional 15–30 minutes until done. Re-check temperature with thermometer before removing from grill.

3   For the oven: Heat oven to 375F and roast chicken in a pan standing up for 45 minutes to an hour or until the thigh reads 165F. Remove from heat and serve. Makes 1 roasted chicken or 4 servings.

Grilled Oysters with Bacon and Butter

SINCE MOVING TO Louisiana, I have had endless opportunities to visit the coast and witness oyster farming firsthand. Although oysters are considered healthiest when eaten raw on the half shell, I love the flavor of grilled oysters with decadent dressings like bacon and butter.

One of the easiest and most satisfying ways to prepare oysters is straight off the grill. Grilling oysters adds subtle smokiness to their naturally silken flavor and can be dressed in a variety of ways. I've seen New Orleans restaurants prepare over-the-top oyster recipes by going as far as to deep-fry the oyster meat, dress it in barbeque sauce, and serve it with blue cheese. Although I think these variations taste wonderful, I'm a huge fan of simple grilled oysters dressed lightly in bacon and butter.

Special equipment needed: grill and heating equipment, thick gloves, and oyster knife or butter knife.

½ pound bacon, speared on grill spears

2 tablespoons parsley, chopped fine

24–36 whole live Louisiana oysters (the larger the better for grilling)

1 stick salted butter, melted

hot sauce, to taste

lemons, quartered for garnishing plates

1   Spear bacon on grill spears and finely chop parsley. Whether using a coal or gas grill, heat grill bed before placing oysters and speared bacon on cleaned grates. If you don't have room, blacken the speared bacon before cooking the oysters. Cool bacon and crush into tiny pieces.

2   Evenly place oysters along the grates of the grill and close lid. Check oysters at 5 minutes to see if the shells have started to "smile" or open. If some are open and some are closed, remove the smiling oysters from the heat and close lid to allow for 2 more minutes for remaining oysters to open.

3 While the remaining oysters are cooking, use a thick oven mitt and an oyster knife (if you have it) or a butter knife to open the shells completely. Discard top shells and plate the oysters in their bottom half shells.

4 Check grill for the last batch of oysters and open. If some of the oysters did not open while grilling, discard and do not eat.

5 Dress oysters: Drizzle open-faced oysters with melted butter and sprinkle with parsley and blackened crisped bacon bits. If you're a fan of hot sauce, add a couple of drops of hot sauce per oyster and serve with lemon wedges. Makes 24–36 grilled oysters.

SIDE DISHES

Artichokes with Red Pepper Aioli

YOU MIGHT NOT be surprised to find that I love my greens. Spinach? Love it. Zucchini? Love it. Edamame? Love it. Artichokes? *Really* love them.

But I am not of the many. As TV commercials for "Hidden Valley Ranch" and finicky five-year-olds everywhere tell us, most Americans can't eat a celery stick without first dipping it into a vat of manufactured ranch.

To these people, I say, "Okay, let's do this." Let's try a clearly delicious roasted vegetable that goes hand-in-hand with a beautiful dip that doesn't come from a plastic bottle, but is made in your own kitchen. If you must dip that celery stick, broccoli, raw vegetable, or whatever it may be into something, why not make it a beautiful red aioli?

Fresh aioli whipped from egg yolks and olive oil is definitely worth a try. I must admit that although I like my veggies just fine, this is one sauce I can't help dipping into.

ARTICHOKES

2–3 large artichokes

1 lemon, halved

This recipe is adapted from Sommer Collier at A Spicy Perspective. Her food blog is indeed a caliente variation of most home-cooked meals and a food blog worth bookmarking. For the original version of her aioli recipe, see the list of reliable online resources in the back of this book. Special equipment needed: a steaming basket.

1   Place a large pot with a steaming basket over high heat and warm. Meanwhile, wash artichokes and cut off the sharp pointy tips of the artichoke leaves. Taking a lemon, squeeze fresh lemon juice over all of the tips to prevent browning. Add artichokes to steaming basket.

2   Steam artichokes for 30–40 minutes or until a center leaf pulls out easily. Remove artichokes from heat.

AIOLI

1 red pepper, thinly sliced and roasted in 1 tablespoon olive oil

½ teaspoon salt, plus more to taste

pepper, to taste

2 egg yolks

2 garlic cloves, minced or pressed

1 teaspoon cayenne, or homemade chili powder (can add less for a less spicy aioli)

½ cup vegetable or olive oil

3 Thinly slice red pepper and roast with olive oil, salt, and pepper to taste until tender. Add red pepper to food processor with egg yolks, garlic, cayenne, and salt. Process until smooth. It's best to process aioli right before your artichokes are ready, otherwise you'll need to refrigerate the sauce.

4 Serve steamed artichokes with fresh red pepper aioli. Makes 2–3 servings.

Stuffed Mushrooms

STUFFED MUSHROOMS WITH Parmesan and fresh herbs never fail to please any of my dinner guests.

The combination of fresh mushrooms with herbs, Parmesan, and olive oil make for a simple appetizer or hardier side dish that, like any other menu item, can make just the right impression with its texture of roasted mushroom caps and tasty filling of cheese, bread, and herbs. Prepare as a vegetarian side dish with the meaty flavor of Portobello mushrooms and you'll have a clearly delicious side dish in no time.

I love the hardiness of Portobello mushrooms but regular white button mushrooms work well also. Looking to use extra herbs from your spring garden? Add mint, basil, or rosemary to the stuffing mixture for even more complexity and flavor.

25–30 small Portobello mushrooms, de-stemmed

½ cup fresh Parmesan, freshly grated (*not* canned Parmesan)

2 garlic cloves, pressed or minced

½ cup bread crumbs

salt and pepper, to taste

1 tablespoon thyme, chopped fine

2 tablespoons parsley, chopped

⅓ cup olive oil

1 Preheat oven to 400F. Gather mushrooms (preferably around 25–30) and de-stem.

2 Combine Parmesan, garlic, bread crumbs, salt, pepper, thyme, and parsley in a bowl. Mix to integrate fully. Drizzle with ⅓ cup olive oil and stir until the entire mixture is wet.

3 Drizzle baking sheet with olive oil. Stuff mushrooms: Spoon a teaspoon of mixture into mushroom hollows (feel free to overstuff). Place stuffed mushrooms on baking sheet, filling side up.

4 Cook until mushrooms are tender and fillings are golden, about 25 minutes. Makes 25–30 mushrooms, or 5–6 servings.

Glazed Honey Shrimp Skewers

ONE OF THE fabulous lessons we cooks learn when it comes to preparing shrimp is the flavor-inducing power of a good marinade. Combine marinated shellfish with the smokiness of your grill and these shrimp pack a seriously sweet and savory punch. I love using honey to marinate shrimp as it begins to caramelize when exposed to the heat of the grill. For this recipe, I suggest larger-size shrimp if available (sizes 15 and 20 per pound), as secure skewering comes down to size. However, smaller-size shrimp will work well for this recipe also (so long as skewering them doesn't destroy their structure).

6 tablespoons amber honey

2 tablespoons soy sauce

1 pound shrimp, large count 15 or 20 per pound

salt and pepper, to taste

1 lime, quartered

1 In a large bowl, whisk together honey and soy sauce with a fork. Toss shrimp in mixture and season with salt and pepper. Marinate refrigerated shrimp for at least an hour to trap in more flavor.

2 For the grill: Skewer shrimp making sure to reserve the leftover marinade. Grill shrimp directly over high heat for about 2–3 minutes per side. Flip, brush with remaining marinade, and grill for an additional 2–3 minutes.

3 Plate Honey Shrimp Skewers with quartered limes. Makes 2–3 servings.

Be wary of overcooking as shrimp exposed to heat for long periods of time develops a rubbery and sometimes fishy taste. It is always good to familiarize yourself with your grill's quirks and temperatures.

Green Beans with Almonds

EVERY GREAT SPRING meal deserves a vibrant, fresh, and healthy side that complements the flavors of Gulf seafood dishes like my Seared Ahi Tuna or Grilled Oysters. Often treated as a little something more to keep dinner guests full—a lagniappe—side dishes like these green beans with almonds celebrate late spring vegetables while reinventing the concept of the side dish.

Green beans grow wonderfully in southern Louisiana so long as they are planted after the last frost and continually until early May. The LSU Ag Center suggests planting bush snaps and all-American selections that will start to appear at farmers' markets in late spring. For planting and especially for eating, my favorite bean to grow is a sweet snap pea, but you can substitute any regular green bean with a semi-thick shell for this recipe.

Slow-roasted in good quality olive oil, garlic, and lemon, these beans have an entrée-like body as they fill the sides of your guests' plates.

1 tablespoon butter, for greasing pan

2 pounds fresh green beans, tips trimmed

½ cup shaved almonds

3–4 cloves garlic, minced or pressed

salt and pepper, to taste

2 tablespoons olive oil

1 lemon, juiced, plus zest

1 Preheat oven to 375F. Line a baking sheet with aluminum foil and grease with butter. Wash green beans, trim ends, and spread across baking sheet. Sprinkle with almonds, garlic, salt, pepper, olive oil, lemon juice, and lemon zest. Bake for 25–30 minutes or until beans are tender, making sure to stir beans at about 15 minutes.

2 Remove from oven and serve. Makes 8 servings.

Roasted Red Potatoes with Rosemary

LIGHTER SPRING DISHES like oysters insist upon masterful sides that can be dressed up or down depending on the level of casualness of your home-cooked meal. I've met only one person who didn't care for potatoes, and I'm certain if they tried these easy stovetop slow-roasted red potatoes with rosemary, they'd have a serious change of heart.

Like fall, spring is one of those in-between temperate periods where I bounce between hot and cold dishes alongside the changing weather. One evening, I may want something cool and refreshing, and another, I may crave warming foods like these easy roasted red potatoes with vibrant rosemary. The beauty in fragrant herbs like rosemary is their hardiness—available in most Louisiana gardens all the year round, rosemary becomes even more robust in the spring when warm temperatures reanimate once cold herb beds.

Roast red potatoes until tender in broth, olive oil, and rosemary for a flavorful vegetable side anyone will love.

Because the fragrance of this particular herb is so strong, you seldom want too much rosemary, but given the 5-pound quantity suggested here, 3–4 tablespoons really is necessary for infusing that natural earthy flavor.

5 pounds red potatoes, washed

2–3 cups chicken broth

3 tablespoons rosemary, chopped fine

salt and pepper, to taste

1 tablespoon chili powder, optional

2–3 tablespoons rosemary or basil olive oil like the one from Vom Fass

fresh rosemary sprigs, for garnishing

1 Wash potatoes and place in an oversized pot, preferably a Dutch oven. Fill Dutch oven with barely enough chicken broth to cover the potatoes. Season with rosemary, salt and pepper, and chili powder (if using). Add half of your olive oil now, retaining the rest for right before potatoes are done cooking.

2 Heat pot over medium high and bring to a light boil. Reduce heat to medium and cook potatoes covered for 45 minutes or until done, stirring occasionally.

3 Right before potatoes are tender—to where, when pierced with a fork, they can almost mash—the broth should be reduced down to almost nothing. At this point, add your remaining olive oil to the pan, stir to coat, and reduce heat to medium-low cooking for an additional 10 minutes. If there isn't any broth in the pan, add ½–1 cup water so that potatoes stay moist and don't burn on bottom.

4 Drain potatoes and garnish with rosemary branches, cracked pepper, and kosher salt. Makes 8–10 servings.

Your potatoes will be more tender and evenly cooked if you use a Dutch oven.

DESSERTS

Lemon Cake with Lemon Buttercream Icing

"YOU DON'T REALLY have a baby shower for your second baby," my good friend Ellen explained to me one night as she rubbed her belly.

Although I'll be the first to admit that I don't know much about baby etiquette or how the proper parental world works, I still couldn't believe the words coming out of my friend's mouth—a baby and no shower? Who wouldn't want to celebrate Ellen's second child with some kind of party? I promptly volunteered to host Ellen's second baby "celebration" (note the switch in jargon) despite only knowing that babies use diapers and drink milk, and, having formerly been one, that they turn into rather interesting human beings with an affinity for food.

Plus, I really wanted an excuse to bake Ellen a cake.

Spring in Baton Rouge is one of my favorite seasons—everything turns green, certain fruits come into season, and the atmosphere feels perfect for a friend's newborn baby. Sensations like these inspire the best of recipes and wanting something fresh, light, and spring-like, I jumped on the opportunity to make a basic vanilla lemon cake with buttercream icing (one of Ellen's favorites) with a tangy but sweet citrus aftertaste. Lemon seemed just right for this occasion as it spreads coolness in our increasingly warm weather and is the perfect combination of tart and sweet. The winter citrus season may be over, but spring dishes taste just wonderful with lemons.

Although I feel that this particular cake goes best on such springy, warm, family occasions, I think that a Lemon Buttercream Cake would do well at wedding showers, kids' birthdays, or just to treat yourself on any warm day. Try this easy, basic vanilla cake recipe infused with lemon juice and lemon rind for a clearly delicious baking experience!

This recipe is adapted from a traditional vanilla cake recipe I've relied on for a while. I added the juice of one lemon (about ¼ cup lemon juice) to a basic homemade buttercream icing and the zest of an entire lemon to the cake batter with 2 tablespoons lemon juice.

A word on Sprinkles: I was first inspired to make this cake after seeing a fantastic recipe by a food blogger named Heather Baird at Sprinkle Bakes. Check out her designs by referring to the online resources index in the back of this book.

CAKE

2 sticks (1 cup) unsalted butter, softened

2 cups sugar

4 large eggs, room temperature

2 teaspoons pure vanilla extract

zest of one lemon

2 tablespoons lemon juice

2 cups buttermilk, well shaken

1 teaspoon salt

2 teaspoons baking powder

1½ teaspoons baking soda

4 cups + 2 tablespoons cake flour (non-self-rising)

1   Preheat oven to 350F. Grease and flour three 9-inch baking rounds.

2   In a standing mixer, cream together butter and sugar until light and fluffy. Add eggs to mixture with vanilla, lemon juice, lemon zest, and buttermilk. Mix to integrate, making sure to scrape down sides of the bowl.

3   Slowly add dry ingredients: Salt, baking powder, baking soda, and then flour last. Remember, the flour should be added in gradual increments, not all at once! As Alton Brown says, "Speed Kills," and he was referring to *cake.*

4   Pour batter into three greased cake pans—this recipe can easily be two layers, but I went with three, so pour into cake pans with enough batter left over for the third layer.

5   Bake for 25–30 minutes per layer (it will be longer if you're going with 2 layers, such as 35–40 minutes). Remove cake from oven when golden brown and a toothpick comes out clean. Allow cakes to rest in their pans for several minutes before transferring to a cooling rack (you don't want the cakes to sit in the pan too long as they'll both continue to bake and potentially get soggy on bottom because of built-up condensation). Cool cakes completely.

ICING

2½ to 3 sticks butter, room temperature

4½ cups confectioner's sugar

½ cup cream

juice of one lemon (about ¼ cup lemon juice; add more if consistency is too dry)

6   Prepare icing: Cream together butter and confectioner's sugar in a standing mixer. Add cream and lemon juice until you have the right consistency (this step is based on personal preference) and the frosting is as tart and lemony as you would like. If it's too tart, add more sugar.

7   Plate bottom layer of cake and frost. My technique is to add a big lump of frosting and smooth evenly. Cakes are highly prone to crumbling, so if you start off with a lot of frosting, you're less likely to upset the cake's texture or structure by getting those nasty crumbs in your frosting. Plus, you can always scrape off excess frosting easily. Add second layer of cake and repeat. Add third layer of cake and repeat.

8   Frost the tops and sides using a similar heavy hand with your lemon buttercream icing. This way, you'll continue to avoid the "crumbs in frosting" problem many at-home cooks experience.

9   Decorate cake. I love sprinkles and think they're so much fun, so I created my own combination of five sprinkles for this occasion. But, if you have fewer resources in your kitchen, you should check out sprinkle variations available at Sprinkle Bakes listed in the online resources in the back index. Makes 12–15 servings.

Strawberry Pavlova with Chocolate

EVERY SPRING, THE Ponchatoula Strawberry Festival proudly displays local crops of the most beautiful red fruits Louisiana has to offer. After a long winter, strawberry crops represent a welcome, long-awaited friend, suggesting both the oncoming of summer and the fruit dishes local chefs will be imagining for the next few months.

There is a certain taken-for-grantedness of Pavlova. It looks so elegant, so fancy, so very bistro-like that many chefs avoid such fancy desserts if only for the fear of ruining the dish in all of its grandeur. But the best part about Pavlova is that it's relatively easy to make—a bed of egg-white meringue topped with whipped cream, sliced strawberries, and dark chocolate demands little time in preparation (although you will have to wait a couple of hours while your meringue sets in the oven). But the results are worth all of its confectionery grandeur.

Spring is also a great time for locally laid organic eggs. For the spring cook, try meringue made from this fantastic resource cross-referenced in the grocers' section at the back of this book (see both online grocers and list of farmers' markets). If using organic, expect an even tastier meringue.

I was inspired to recreate this Strawberry Pavlova with Chocolate after having lunch with my friend Melanie in downtown Baton Rouge. A Baton Rouge café named Strands offers small menus with major culinary punch. A family business, Strands prides itself on two chefs—Blanchard and Mon—who studied at the *patisserie res* at Le Cordon Bleu Sydney, Australia. If you're looking for a proper English tea, or yes, even this Strawberry Pavlova, Strands is a must for the hungry seasonal chef.

4 organic large egg whites

pinch of salt

½ teaspoon white vinegar

¾ cup sugar

1 tablespoon cornstarch (can use cream of tartar)

1 teaspoon vanilla extract (I prefer a combination of half vanilla, half almond)

1–2 cups fresh Louisiana strawberries, stemmed and sliced thin

3 ounces dark chocolate

2 tablespoons heavy cream

whipped cream, for garnishing

strawberries, thinly sliced, for garnishing

1   Preheat oven to 350F. Place egg whites, salt, and vinegar in a standing mixer and beat on high until soft peaks form. In a separate bowl, combine ¾ cup sugar with the cornstarch and add to egg whites mixture in three separate installments, beating after each addition to integrate fully. Slowly add vanilla extract (and almond if using) and beat on high until stiff peaks form.

2   Line baking sheet with parchment paper or a Silpat mat to prevent meringue from sticking and spoon into 8 big mounds with 1 inch between spoonfuls. Bake for 10 minutes, lower heat to 200F, and bake for one hour. Turn off oven and prop door open slightly allowing meringues to cool inside for another hour. As with baking a cheesecake, meringue should be tempered throughout the baking process.

3   Right before serving, melt dark chocolate with heavy cream. Plate meringue and dress with whipped cream, melted chocolate, and sliced strawberries. Makes 8 servings.

Glazed Tarte aux Baies
(French Berry Tart)

"THIS IS THE best thing you've ever made me. Seriously. Maybe it's because I'm partial to fruit tarts, but I have to say, out of everything you've ever cooked . . . EVER . . . this is the best thing I've tried," Jonathan says, fork digging deep into the side of this fresh Glazed Tarte aux Baies (berry tart).

And Jonathan should know. He's been on the receiving end of dozens of recipes for Clearly Delicious and has quite the discriminating palette.

"Even better than the pesto you like so much?" I ask, insistent.

"Way better than the pesto. And I *love* your pesto," Jonathan persists.

All that for a French berry tart? I must say, even I'm impressed with the way Jonathan responded to this dish. He's not one for hiding his feelings about food and yet, he can't stop licking the yellow custard from his fingers and picking off large chunks of strawberries.

The beautiful berry tarts made popular in French provincial cooking inspire this recipe. In one of my very first Clearly Delicious posts, I "ummed" and "awed" at the price of a gorgeous flavorful $30 French tart at a local bakery. As it turns out, the same treat can be made at home—quite easily—and for under $10 with fresh spring produce.

Normally, I'd use Jonathan's words to tie this recipe into some larger point or purpose—how fruit tarts are a perfect end to any spring meal. But today, I think this provincial-style berry tart can speak for itself. Filled with fresh spring strawberries, ripe fruits, and rich homemade custard, this Glazed Tarte aux Baies is as beautiful is it is flavorful. As memorable as it is memory making. As Great as it is Grape-filled (sorry, I appear to be reaching here).

Let's just say, this tart may very well be the best, most Clearly Delicious dish I've ever made. Ever.

ALMOND CRUST

½ cup almond meal (see recipe in "Cooking Methods, Techniques, and Food Preservation")

2 cups all-purpose flour

¾ cup (1½ sticks) unsalted butter

⅔ cup confectioner's sugar

1 egg

1 teaspoon salt

1 teaspoon vanilla extract

1 teaspoon almond extract

FILLING

4 egg yolks

½ cup granulated sugar

3 tablespoons cornstarch

2 cups skim milk, can use whole

¼ cup (½ stick) unsalted butter

½ teaspoon vanilla extract

½ teaspoon almond extract

Optional: Sliced pineapple, grapes, mandarin oranges, and/or any other favorite seasonal fruit such as fresh cherries

1   Prepare the crust: Add almond meal to all-purpose flour and whisk to combine in a large bowl. In a standing mixer (I use my Kitchenaid), combine flour, butter, sugar, egg, salt, and vanilla and almond extracts until well blended. Slowly sift in flour and almond mixture to this wet mixture. Mix until fully combined. Refrigerate for at least 2 hours before rolling out.

2   Prepare the custard/filling: Whisk together egg yolks, ¼ cup sugar, and cornstarch.

3   In a large, nonstick saucepan, whisk ¼ cup sugar (the last of the sugar) with 2 cups milk and bring to a boil, stir occasionally.

4   Once milk and sugar mixture is boiling, pour ¼ of the milk mixture into your whisked egg mixture to "temper" the wet ingredients, stirring constantly while you perform this step. Remove milk mixture from heat and slowly add the egg mixture into the milk one (saucepan). Return this wet mixture to medium-high heat and whisk until the cream thickens and comes to a complete boil.

5   Remove thickened custard from heat and add butter and vanilla and almond extract, stirring until the butter is melted completely and integrated. Transfer custard to a bowl and refrigerate covered until ready to construct the pie.

6   Cook the pie crust: Preheat oven to 350F and flour a clean surface. Remove dough from refrigerator and roll out onto floured surface. The dough will be hard and cold, so it may take several minutes for you to get it to do as you want during this step. However, this firmness is a good sign—all good pie crusts are hard to work with at first, and persistence always yields a great crust.

TOPPING

2 cups fresh strawberries

1 cup fresh raspberries

1 cup fresh blueberries

3 kiwis, peeled and sliced

1 cup red jelly

7   Roll out dough to the size of your pan and add to a nonstick, loose-bottom tart pan. Press crust into tart pan, cut off excess dough, and puncture the bottom of the pie dough fully with a fork. Save the leftover dough for a future tart.

8   Line pie dough with aluminum foil and fill with either ceramic oven-safe weights or dry bean weights.

9   Bake pie crust for 25 minutes or until golden brown. Remove crust from oven and cool completely.

10   When ready to construct the tart—it's best when constructed just before serving—prep your topping ingredients. Halve strawberries, wash raspberries and blueberries, and slice any extra fruit you may be using (such as kiwi or pineapple).

11   Fill pie crust with refrigerated custard and top with mixed fruit. I decorated my tart in circular rounds, but really this step is an aesthetic choice.

12   Once pie is decorated, add jelly to a nonstick skillet and heat on medium-high until jelly has melted fully. Using a silicone pastry brush, paint fruit with the jelly. Serve immediately. Makes 12 servings.

It is of the utmost importance that you remove the milk mixture from the heat of the stovetop when adding your egg mixture. The eggs function as the thickening agent, but they're still eggs. If you do this step too slowly and over a heat that's too high, the eggs will instantly cook upon hitting your boiling milk and you'll be left with a chunky custard that still tastes great, but will have large fat molecules throughout. If these chunks do occur, strain the custard through a mesh kitchen strainer to fix the problem.

Strawberry Cake with Strawberry Buttercream Frosting

EVERYONE IN LOUISIANA loves strawberries.

And it's no surprise this time of year—they're everywhere. With the Ponchatoula Strawberry Festival—a free annual fundraiser for charitable organizations—taking place in early spring, strawberries are popping up everywhere and I find my brain buzzing from the endless recipe options out there.

Strawberry shortcake, strawberry pie, strawberry crêpes with Nutella, strawberry French toast, strawberry scones, strawberry parfaits, strawberry muffins, strawberry almond tarts, and the best? Just strawberries by themselves.

Something about the Louisiana heat makes strawberries sweeter, brighter, redder, and yes, better. Better than the strawberries I've had anywhere else.

In a sense, I guess you can have greener grass (albeit in the form of redder strawberries) in southern Louisiana.

Several weeks ago, when the strawberries first started rearing their heads at my local produce market, I found myself dreaming of making flaming strawberries like the ones at Sprinkle Bakes (see online resources index in the back of this book) and concocting a dessert item that wasn't just shortcake.

Luckily, my friend Andrew celebrated his twenty-fourth birthday this year, just in time for me to experiment with a strawberry cake.

I used two quarts fresh strawberries to get the light pink hues and fruity flavor of the cake itself. This recipe is a culinary discovery of sorts. It's incredibly hard to find a recipe for Strawberry Cake made from scratch. Most home cooks rely on baking mixes with freeze-dried strawberries and artificial flavors, but my recipe uses fresh strawberries and is as easy as those box mixes although there are a couple of additional steps. You'll never use store-bought strawberry cake mixes again!

Needless to say, Andrew was delighted and surprised by my fruit-inspired confection. After the candles were blown out, and the stems licked clean, we dove into this unbelievably (clearly) delicious cake—it tasted like summer, smelled like our child-hoods, and filled up our stomachs so much that the tables nearby at an overcrowded restaurant patio looked on with bated breath.

Smiling, happy, another year older, Andrew asked me, "How did you know I loved strawberries? Did someone tell you?"

That's easy Andrew, *everyone* loves strawberries.

CAKE

2 quarts fresh Louisiana strawberries (will yield about 2 cups fresh strawberry puree, half for the cake and half for the icing)

2¾ cups cake flour

1 cup all-purpose flour

2½ teaspoons baking powder

¾ teaspoon salt

2 sticks unsalted butter, room temperature

2½–2¾ cup sugar, to taste

1 tablespoon vanilla extract

1 tablespoon almond extract

8 egg whites

½ cup skim milk; can use whole

1 Preheat oven to 350F. Grease two baking sheets and set aside. Wash two quarts fresh Louisiana strawberries, de-stem, and add to a food processor. Using the blade attachment, process strawberries into a puree.

2 Mix dry ingredients in a large bowl with a whisk: Cake flour, all-pur-pose flour, baking powder, and salt. Set aside.

3 Using a standing mixer and paddle attachment, beat butter and sugar on medium-high until mixture is light and fluffy. Add vanilla and almond extract and mix to integrate. Slowly add egg whites to mixture using the lowest speed; scrape down sides of the bowl after each addition.

4 In another bowl, combine 1 cup strawberry puree with ½ cup milk. Gradually add dry ingredients to standing mixture, alternating be-tween additions of strawberry mixture and dry ingredients until all have been combined with the batter. Scrape down sides of the bowl and mix one last time.

5 Pour ⅓ of batter into each of three greased 9-inch cake pans, or ½ mixture into each of two greased 9-inch cake pans.

FROSTING

2½ sticks butter, room temperature

4½ cups confectioner's sugar

½ cup heavy cream

¼–½ cup reserved fresh strawberry puree; can use more if frosting is too thick or dry

6 Bake for 25–30 minutes per layer. It will be longer if you're going with two layers (around 35–40 minutes). Remove cake from oven when golden brown and a toothpick comes out clean. Allow cakes to rest in their pans for several minutes before transferring to a cooling rack (you don't want the cakes to sit in the pan too long as they'll continue to bake and potentially get soggy on bottom because of built-up condensation). Cool cakes completely.

7 Prepare frosting: Cream together butter and confectioner's sugar in a standing mixer. Add strawberry puree until you have the right consistency and the frosting is as sweet and strawberry-like as you prefer (this step is based on personal preference).

8 Construct cake: Plate bottom layer of cake on a serving dish and frost. See Lemon Buttercream Cake recipe at the beginning of this desserts section for how to frost like a professional and avoid crumbs in your frosting.

9 Decorate cake: For this particular occasion, I went with more fresh strawberries quartered on the sides and top. Makes 12–15 servings.

Fruit Salad Bake with Curry

MY FAVORITE DESSERTS for spring often require little baking. Aside from my sister buttercream fruit cakes—the Lemon Buttercream Cake that opens the spring desserts section or the Strawberry Buttercream Cake that precedes this recipe—great spring desserts are inspired by nature itself. Fresh berries and whole fruits with just a hint of whipped cream always leave me happier and more satisfied after a heavy meal than any bakery concoction.

For this recipe, I was motivated by a delicious canned fruit bake with curry I had at a friend's house one year, but I've adapted her presentation to include seasonally available fruits. When necessary, canned fruits can offer a faster and cheaper alternative that is still delicious, but I always err on the side of fresh produce as often as possible. Here, a combination of fresh nectarines, apricots, and pineapple make for a spring favorite fruit bake that can easily be adjusted to your respective season with summer, fall, or winter fruits.

1 pound apricots, halved

1 pound nectarines, quartered

1 fresh pineapple, cubed

1 pint blueberries, washed

1 tablespoon brown sugar

1 teaspoon cinnamon

1 teaspoon curry powder (yellow)

½ teaspoon nutmeg

1 teaspoon allspice

1 Preheat oven to 350F. Meanwhile, halve apricots, quarter nectarines, cube pineapple, and wash blueberries. Layer fresh fruit into an oven-proof casserole dish that has been sprayed with nonstick cooking spray. Sprinkle fruit with brown sugar, cinnamon, curry, nutmeg, and allspice.

2 Bake for 30 minutes or until fruit is tender and juices are abundant. Serve warm with whipped cream, ice cream, or by itself. Makes 8–10 servings.

Savory Crêpes Boudin

IN THE OPENING to his food memoir *The Sweet Life in Paris*, food writer and chef David Lebovitz writes that he (officially) knew he was becoming a Parisian the morning he performed an elaborate ritual just to take out his trash. He changed from his otherwise comfortable lounge clothes into dressy slacks for fear that any of his neighbors might see him wearing traditionally American Saturday morning apparel. Lebovitz's argument is that it was not what he wore, but that he chose to change just to take out the garbage that suggests a complete transformation from an American mindset to a Parisian one.

This recipe has nothing to do with household chores, but everything to do with mindset. I can remember how bizarrely I looked upon Boudin the first time I saw it. *Boudin blanc*—the kind of gray-ish variety most commonly sold in southern Louisiana—combines pork and rice in a "dressing" or dirty rice. Stuffed inside intestine casings (sometimes synthetic casings, but usually pig's intestines), Boudin had a flavor that astounded me with the tenderness to be found inside. Really, Boudin tastes nothing like your traditional sausage.

The day I knew I considered Louisiana home must have been when I bought a package of Boudin—not knowing what recipe I'd use it for—but that I would be using it for *something*. I have since put Boudin on everything from the pizza recipe in the summer section to omelets and these crêpes. Not a traditional French filling by any means, the addition of Boudin suggests a similar Louisiana take on a French classic making for an omelet that is entirely Louisiana.

The batter to this recipe will make 6–8 very large crêpes. Although any nonstick skillet will work here, a real crêpe is prepared on a Le Creuset nonstick flat skillet. See the Equipment List in the opening of this book for why I endorse this kitchen item and just how great it makes the end result. As for the recipe itself, many thanks go to a chance encounter with a fabulous French chef from Lyon for her "Crêpes Marion" version adapted here.

CRÊPE BATTER

a dozen brown eggs, beaten

6¼ cups whole milk

pinch of salt

1 stick of salted butter, softened

1 tablespoon rum, orange-flavored water, or Grand Marnier

1 ⅓ cups sugar

4–4½ cups all-purpose flour

FILLING

1 cup cherry tomatoes, halved

½ cup spinach

1 Boudin link

3 green onions, chopped

1 tablespoon freshly chopped parsley

salt and pepper, to taste

1 cup Brie, thinly sliced

1 cup tomato sauce

1   Prepare crêpe batter: Mix beaten eggs, milk, salt, rum or orange-flavored water, butter, sugar, and flour in a bowl.

2   Heat a flat skillet with butter and add ½ cup crêpe batter to the pan. Cook until bottom is golden brown. Flip, and cook the other side until done. Reduce heat to medium-low until cooked through. Repeat.

3   While the crêpe batter is cooking, prepare filling batter in a separate skillet: Combine tomato, spinach, Boudin, green onions, parsley, salt and pepper, and cook until done, or until vegetables have lightly browned. Add tomato sauce, mix to integrate, and heat for one to two minutes more. Remove from heat.

4   Add filling to crêpe and sprinkle with Brie. Fold crêpe over the top and sit in skillet at low heat for 1–2 minutes for cheese to melt.

5   Plate crêpe and repeat. Makes 6–8 large crêpes.

Refrigerate batter for two hours before using (the French tradition), but you can use batter immediately.

Mango Salsa, recipe on page 23

Above: Peeled Zucchini and Asparagus Salad with Spicy Wasabi, recipe on page 29

Left: Petite Crab Cakes with Cajun Dipping Sauce, recipe on page 24

Strawberry Brie Bruschetta, recipe on page 28

Antipasti Avocado Asparagus Salad, recipe on page 30

Pizza Florentine, recipe on page 33

Seared Ahi Tuna, recipe on page 35

Above: Bowtie Spinach Pesto Pasta with Wild Mushrooms, recipe on page 36

Right: Stuffed Mushrooms, recipe on page 42

Strawberry Pavlova with Chocolate, recipe on page 50

Above: Glazed Tarte aux Baies (French Berry Tart), recipe on page 52

Below: Strawberry Cake with Strawberry Buttercream Frosting, recipe on page 55

Lemon Lavender Muffins, recipe on page 66

Black Bean Corn Salsa, recipe on page 76

Above: Sweet Bell Peppers and Cherry Tomatoes

Below: Ciabatta Bread with Herbs and Cheese, recipe on page 192

Red and Yellow Bruschetta, recipe on page 71

Watermelon Radish Crostini with Butter and Sea Salt, recipe on page 73

Bananas Foster Croissant French Toast

AS CRUDE AS it sounds, I don't think any local has ever experienced New Orleans until they've had a decadent, fatty breakfast the morning after having too much to drink. My first breakfast in New Orleans consisted of creamy eggs Benedict and several forkfuls of French Toast Foster I shared with a friend at Stanley's on Jackson Square. For someone who had never experienced Bananas Foster, I was alarmed that dessert could so easily be a breakfast item in the city—as the dish is commonly served with a scoop of vanilla ice cream—but it was certainly something I could get behind.

There are about as many ways to make French toast as there are bakers to imagine it. Here, I suggest using croissants for the "toast" component, but any good-quality baguette or bread will be equally as lovely. Although you can make Bananas Foster several ways, the one that impresses any brunch guest most is the candy-like variation made with buttery French croissants. Toasted in a warm batter of heavy cream, nutmeg, and vanilla, this French toast begs for a decadent helping of caramel syrup and a scoop of *real* ice cream—whether this dish is eaten after a night of one too many drinks or not.

FRENCH TOAST AND BATTER

3 eggs

1 cup heavy cream

1 teaspoon cinnamon

½ teaspoon nutmeg

1 tablespoon vanilla extract

6 large croissants, halved

butter, for greasing pan

1 Prepare batter mixture: Beat together eggs, cream, cinnamon, nutmeg, and vanilla extract. Reserve for dipping croissants.

2 Halve croissants. Warm a large nonstick skillet over medium-high heat and grease pan with butter. Dip croissant halves in batter mixture and fork out of bowl allowing the croissant half to drip for several seconds removing any excess batter. Add to hot pan and cook for three minutes on each side or until golden brown. Plate croissants when done.

BANANA FOSTER SYRUP

⅛ cup molasses

½ cup brown sugar, firmly packed

1 cup maple syrup

1–2 teaspoons vanilla or almond
extract

1 cup Bourbon Candied Pecans,
recipe in the Winter Appetizers
section

4 bananas, cut into circular rounds

3   Prepare bananas and Banana Foster Syrup: Cut 4 bananas into circular rounds and reserve for French toast. In a large nonstick skillet, whisk together molasses, brown sugar, maple syrup, candied pecans, and extract. Bring to a light simmer and reduce heat for two to three minutes on low. Remove from heat after syrup has had time to simmer and reduce. Dress croissant halves in Banana Foster Syrup and top with fresh banana slices and vanilla ice cream. Serve immediately. Makes 4–6 servings.

Absinthe (a New Orleans tradition)

MY FIRST TIME drinking absinthe in New Orleans took place with a "real-life pirate" at a bar off Jackson Square. I use the term "real-life pirate" here as locals have told me that they are *not* street performers, but participants in a garb-specific lifestyle choice. Only in New Orleans can you find actual "Pirate's Alleys" specializing in antique-distilled absinthe and the ambiance of nineteenth-century absinthe houses. If you ever find yourself in Jackson Square looking for a peculiarly good time, take the small alley to the left of St. Louis Cathedral, walk a block, and enjoy this blissful beverage complete with green fairies and, well, pirates.

Pirate's Alley (recently renamed "The Olde Absinthe House") takes absinthe seriously—specializing in four varieties of absinthe, the house is always ready to serve its crystalline cubes and slotted spoons. They sit out on the counter beckoning you to order not wine, not beer, but absinthe.

Much of the romance behind absinthe lies in the preparation ritual popularized in nineteenth-century Europe. The pouring of the liquor over the sugar cube, the flaming sugar cube and its watering down create an impressive presentation and drink (for a complete list of the available varieties of popular absinthe that I've used with this recipe, see the resources index in the back of this book).

At The Olde Absinthe House, $10 will get you a middle-shelf absinthe with Absente Liqueur. For the big spender and tourist, $20 will get you the fanciest and most specialized of absinthes distilled locally—Absinthe Superior Nouvelle Orléans made in a 130-year-old New Orleans absinthe still with a rum-liqueur base. It's twice the price, but a taste of New Orleans history and flavor.

So, sit back, relax, and have a nice chat with your new Pirate friend as you enjoy the sweet licorice tastes of absinthe. You might even see the green fairy. After all, you're already seeing pirates!

Special equipment needed: absinthe glass and spoon.

TRADITIONAL ABSINTHE

1–3 sugar cubes (depending on how sweet you like your beverage)

3 ounces Absente Liqueur

2½–3 ounces water

1   Place absinthe spoon over a glass ("absinthe glass" if you have it, but a wine glass will work fine here) and top with a sugar cube (can use 1–3 here depending on taste preferences). Pour 3 ounces Absente Liqueur over sugar cube *slowly.*

2   Dissolve the sugar cube with 2½–3 ounces water (preferably from an absinthe fountain). Stir with absinthe spoon and enjoy! Makes 1 serving.

The liquor-doused sugar cube is ready to be set aflame at step one. Do so with caution, but this step may be skipped.

Southern Mint Julep

ALTHOUGH MINT JULEPS are often associated with iconic southern events such as the Kentucky Derby, I have had the best mint juleps not in the French Quarter in New Orleans, but on the outskirts of the quarter at a brick house called, "Bar Tonique" across from Armstrong Park. Here, the art of mixology is a southern treat with everything from fruit juices to infusions to gums and bitters made from scratch. When you order a drink, the bartenders make everything right in front of you and the process takes more than several minutes.

This recipe is my variation of a favorite Bar Tonique beverage, but for more information on the popular local bar, see the list of online resources in the back. Want to make this recipe non-alcoholic? Substitute for 30 ounces bourbon 4 cups of half club soda with half lime juice or simply ginger ale.

Serve Southern Mint Juleps in heavy mason jars for the rustic classic dish of a country dish, using fresh mint leaves that grow beautifully in our early southern gardens before the oppressive heat of summer.

Special equipment needed: old-fashioned mason jars, for serving

⅓ cup mint leaves, packed

10 fresh mint leaves for garnishing

1½ cups water

1½ cups white sugar

30 ounces bourbon, such as Evan Williams Single Barrel Bourbon (what Bar Tonique often serves when preparing its cocktails)

1   Wash mint leaves, making sure to reserve 10 leaves for garnishing. Roughly chop remaining mint leaves and set aside.

2   In a nonstick saucepan, warm water, sugar, and mint, whisking regularly until mixture comes to a boil over medium-high heat. Lower heat slightly and whisk syrup regularly until it reduces by a little less than a third. Remove from heat and bring to room temperature.

3   Strain syrup free from mint leaves using a mesh sifter and use immediately or refrigerate for up to a month (although best if used within the week of preparation).

4   Prepare cocktails: Fill a large pitcher with ice, bourbon, and simple syrup. Stir cocktail and pour into individual mason jars. Dress mason jars with mint sprigs and serve. Makes 6–8 cocktails.

Lemon Lavender Muffins

AFTER A FRIEND of a friend's visit to an open-air market in Savoy, France, I acquired the most fragrant and lovely lavender one spring in Baton Rouge. Although a European-grown variety, the lavender was purple and fragrant like many of the plants available in early spring to local gardeners.

Although the amount was small—only 2 tablespoons of fresh French lavender—the herb could easily be used to infuse lavender olive oil, lavender ice cream, or these Lemon Lavender Muffins.

Use fresh lavender from your garden (or from Savoy if you're so lucky!) for a lemon muffin with a certain "je ne sais quoi." The result is a light, citrusy muffin with a hint of fresh spring herbs.

Special equipment needed: 1 coffee grinder, for grinding the lavender.

2 teaspoons fresh lavender, ground

1 stick butter, softened

1 cup sugar

2 eggs

½ teaspoon salt

1 teaspoon baking powder

½ cup milk

1 tablespoon lemon zest

2 tablespoons lemon juice

1½ cups flour

1   Preheat oven to 350F. Line a 12-muffin pan with cupcake cups. Grind lavender in a coffee grinder.

2   Add softened butter to standing mixer such as a Kitchenaid and turn on low speed. Mix butter for 1–2 minutes, or until butter is fluffy. Add sugar and mix to integrate. Add eggs one at a time.

3   Add salt, baking powder, lavender, milk, lemon zest, and lemon juice to mixture. Mix on low to integrate. Slowly add flour until fully incorporated with wet mixture. Stop mixer to scrape down sides and mix one last minute.

4   Pour batter into muffin pans and bake for 15–20 minutes, or until tops are golden brown and a toothpick comes out clean. Remove from oven and transfer to a cooling pan.

LEMON GLAZE

¼ cup lemon juice

⅓ cup sugar

1 tablespoon honey

5 Create the Lemon Glaze: Combine lemon juice with sugar and honey. Whisk to integrate. Puncture holes throughout tops of the muffins, using a small toothpick. Pour glaze over tops of muffins. It's good to do this last step over a plate that you don't plan on serving the muffins on as you will have lots of glaze pouring off onto the plate. Clean up any glaze that may have gotten stuck to the sides of your muffins. Transfer to a plate and serve. Makes 12 muffins.

summer

JUNE–AUGUST

Some of my favorite Louisiana produce items are the fruits and vegetables readily available during the summer months. Beginning with early June through the month of August, bright red and yellow peppers, ripe avocados, fresh corn, and tender eggplant fill the edges of my plates and the recipes on the following pages. Summer is a great time for yellow squash, zucchini, and those infrequent pints of blackberries and blueberries usually only cultivated at their peak during the months of May and June. For the spices of summer, basil and cilantro grow best in Louisiana's hot summer days (as long as they have *lots* of sun), while crawfish, prosciutto, sausage, and sirloin take the cooking outdoors and onto the grill.

Red and Yellow Bruschetta

Salsa Verde with Sweet Basil and Cilantro

Watermelon Radish Crostini with Butter and Sea Salt

Avocado Egg Rolls with Honey Cilantro Asian
   Dipping Sauce

Black Bean Corn Salsa

Fig and Prosciutto Salad with Goat Cheese and Spinach

Summer Gazpacho with Avocado and Cucumber

Crawfish Étouffée Ravioli with Spicy Cream Sauce

Fig and Prosciutto Pizza with Brie, and Boudin Pizza

Grilled Sausage Bedded with Blackened Summer Squash

Spicy Shrimp Cocktail

Sirloin Steak with Herb Butter and (possibly) Egg

Perfect Guacamole

Blistered Eggplant with Mozzarella

Smoked Salmon Carpaccio with Dill,
   Capers, and Quail Eggs

Corn Bread "Soufflé"

Pasta Salad with Zucchini, Almonds, and Goat Cheese

Fruit Salad with Blood Orange Olive Oil and
   Blueberry Balsamic Dressing

Raspberry Almond Cream Cheese Tartlets

Blueberry Balsamic Gelato

Key Lime Cheesecake Tarts

Banana Pudding

Any-Season Crumble with Apricots and Almonds

Watermelon Juice with Basil

Louisiana Bloody Marys

Louisiana Lemonade, including Pomegranate or
   Strawberry Variation, and Limeade

Watermelon Feta Salad Cakes

APPETIZERS

Red and Yellow Bruschetta

FOODS RICH IN colors are inherently good for you—rich in vitamins A, C, and other natural goodness. Beautiful foods like red and yellow peppers make for a beautiful body.

And summer Louisiana produce couldn't be more beautiful—the markets are filled with brightly colored peppers, tomatoes, and oversized bunches of basil. With such natural food stuffs looking back at me, how could I resist making such a lovely appetizer?

Served on hardy toasted whole wheat bread, this red and yellow bruschetta inspires my stomach to eat healthy rich produce during the summer months. Although a green pepper would substitute just "fine" here, I highly suggest following the below recipe pretty closely—not only are the red and yellow peppers pretty, but they're also noticeably sweet, making for a palate-friendly balance between sweet peppers and a tangy lemon, basil, and olive oil–infused dressing.

With naturally sweet peppers and juicy tomatoes, my red and yellow bruschetta is low fat *and* clearly delicious. Who knew taking care of your body looked—and tasted—so good?

1 red bell pepper, thinly sliced

1 yellow bell pepper, thinly sliced

1 cup cherry tomatoes, halved

½ cup basil, thinly sliced or torn into small pieces

4 cloves garlic, thinly sliced

3 tablespoons olive oil

3 tablespoons lemon juice

2 tablespoons red pepper flakes

whole wheat bread (can substitute French baguette)

olive oil, for toasting bread

salt and pepper, to taste

1 Wash ingredients—peppers, tomatoes, and basil. Peel garlic. Thinly slice seeded peppers, basil, and garlic, then halve cherry tomatoes, and add to a mixing bowl. Toss ingredients with olive oil and lemon juice, red pepper flakes, and salt and pepper to taste. Set aside.

2 In a nonstick skillet, warm enough olive oil to cover the bottom of the pan thinly and add bread. Toast until golden brown and flip to toast other side. Plate bread for dressing.

3 Top with red and yellow bruschetta mixture and serve. Makes 8–10 servings.

Salsa Verde with Sweet Basil and Cilantro

MANY SOUTHERN LOUISIANA chefs know the plight of keeping meals light during the hot summer days and the easiest way to start off a cooling menu is with a sweet or salty salsa.

Salsa Verde is the not-so-redheaded stepchild of the salsa family: made from ripe tomatillos instead of regular red tomatoes, the resulting dip is a beautiful green and, when roasted, the epitome of fresh summer sweetness. Pulse together roasted ripe tomatillos with sweet basil and a large handful of cilantro for one of my favorite greens this summer.

For this simple method, you will need a food processor for combining the salsa into a vibrant green dip. Make sure to roast the tomatillos before processing to condense the fruit into a sweeter, more flavorful ingredient. Although some summer chefs prefer using raw tomatillos because of their natural "tang," my method packs a pleasing sweetness for an already tangy dish.

1 pound tomatillos, halved

salt and pepper, to taste

½ onion, chopped fine

¼ cup cilantro, chopped fine

¼ cup basil, chopped fine

1–2 jalapeño peppers, with or without seeds, chopped fine

pinch of sugar

1   Preheat broiler to high for roasting the tomatillos. Cut tomatillos in half, sprinkle with salt and pepper, and lay flat side down on a lightly oiled baking sheet. Broil for 6–8 minutes, or until skin is lightly blackened. Remove from oven and cool slightly.

2   Chop onion, cilantro, basil, and jalapeño fine. Add to food processor with sugar and roasted tomatillos. Season with salt and pepper and pulse until all ingredients are integrated. Add more salt and pepper to taste and continue to pulse to desired texture.

3   Serve with chips as a dip or with fish as a summer dressing. Makes 10–12 servings.

For an even brighter variation, substitute ½ pound tomatillos with 1 orange and add 2 tablespoons finely chopped mint to the dish. This sweeter salsa verde has a bright citrus-like zest that goes great with chips, but even better as a topping on smoked fish, shrimp, or oysters.

Watermelon Radish Crostini
with Butter and Sea Salt

THE FIRST TIME I ever saw a watermelon radish, I thought I was dreaming. Something about the beautiful interior of this otherwise disregarded root was equal parts cartoonish and equal parts psychedelic. But for a chef, the root was just beautiful.

Often known for their powerful flavor, watermelon radishes can be offset with the addition of kitchen favorites like butter, salt, and bread. Plus, they make for one heck of a presentation.

Although my favorite way to serve this radish is raw, bright, and fresh on a baguette with butter and sea salt (kosher salt if you have it), the radish makes for a lovely topper on any summer salad. Natural neon pink and green colors play off dark greens nicely as when bedded on top of my Summer Gazpacho with Avocado and Cucumber. Or, simply top sliced cucumbers with soft white cheese and a thin slice of this radish for a bread-less appetizer that evokes the colors of summer.

If you've read this far you can catch me in the act: a watermelon radish isn't *necessarily* a "summer" produce item. They grow best in winter and through early spring, but I love the way watermelon radishes recreate my favorite summer fruit (watermelon) in root form. A miscategorized root vegetable indeed, but a summer staple in my kitchen.

3–5 watermelon radishes, washed, stemmed, and thinly sliced

French baguette, cut into vertical slices

unsalted butter, to taste

kosher or sea salt, to taste

1   Wash, stem, and thinly slice watermelon radishes with a sharp paring knife. Set aside. Cut baguette using a bread knife at a vertical angle so that slices are long and diagonal.

2   Butter bread to taste and dress with slices of watermelon radishes. Sprinkle with kosher or sea salt and serve. Makes 12–15 servings.

Avocado Egg Rolls with Honey Cilantro
Asian Dipping Sauce

AVOCADO EGG ROLLS have become a staple in my summer kitchen. The dish is pretty simple: fresh avocado, a diced tomato, and cilantro all mixed with a tiny bit of minced onion and salt, then wrapped in a standard egg roll shell and fried (pan or deep fried). The taste is creamy and warm. What makes the dish even better is the out-of-this-world Honey Cilantro Asian Dipping Sauce with which I serve it. The first time I experimented with the combination of honey and cilantro, I just sat there eating, smiling, and refusing to talk. Avocado Egg Rolls with Honey Cilantro Asian Dipping Sauce is an impressive experience.

I always encourage free-form cooking, but in the case of these egg rolls, I highly suggest using and acquiring all of the ingredients below and not skimping on too many of the spices for the sauce. What makes this dish special is its unique fusion of Asian spices, nuts, and oils that complement the avocado base in the egg rolls. Make these egg rolls as an appetizer with sushi or other Asian cuisines, or double the recipe for a vegetarian meal.

SAUCE

¼ cup olive oil

4 teaspoons white vinegar

3 teaspoons balsamic vinegar

1 teaspoon tamarind

⅓ cup honey

½ teaspoon turmeric

1 teaspoon cumin

⅔ cup fresh cilantro, chopped

1 teaspoon freshly ground black pepper

2 garlic cloves, pressed or minced

1   Prepare the sauce: Add olive oil, vinegars, tamarind, honey, and other spices—turmeric, cumin, cilantro, black pepper, garlic—into a bowl and whisk. Add chopped green onions, sugar, and chopped cashews. Microwave for 1 minute, then use a blender or food processor to puree the mixture. Pour mixture into a serving bowl, stir, and refrigerate (covered) until ready to use.

2 green onions, chopped fine

1 tablespoon sugar

½ cup chopped cashews

EGG ROLLS

2 avocados, pitted and cubed

2 tablespoons onion, chopped

1 tomato, diced

1 tablespoon fresh cilantro, chopped

2 dashes salt

4–6 egg roll wrappers (depending on how much filling your mixture yields)

1 egg, beaten

peanut oil, for frying

2   Prepare the avocado egg roll filling: Put 2 avocados, onion, tomatoes, cilantro, and salt in a bowl. Mix to combine.

3   Lay out 1 egg roll sheet and fill with 2 heaping tablespoons avocado filling (can use more or less based on your personal preference and size of the egg roll sheets).

4   Brush edges with egg yolk, wrap short edges in, and then roll wrap long ways. Prepare around 4–6 egg rolls depending on how much filling your avocados yield and how full you make the rolls.

5   Fry egg rolls: Skillet fry egg rolls in peanut oil until golden brown on both sides. Cook to brown corner edges as well.

6   Transfer to a plate and serve with Asian dipping sauce. Makes 4–6 egg rolls.

See "Cooking Methods, Techniques, and Food Preservation" at the beginning of this book for a more detailed explanation of how to roll an egg roll properly.

Black Bean Corn Salsa

"CORN, 20¢ A PIECE," the sign at my local produce market reads. I grab two bags and begin stuffing them with 10 ears of corn: 10 ears of corn for only $2? I must be in Louisiana.

During the winter months, I tend to go into a foodma (food + coma = foodma). I eat warm soups, gorge myself on sweet breads, and perhaps drink one too many cups of hot coffee. The fresh vegetables of my summertime yearnings stare back at me limp and depressed at every market, and I find myself invoking mirages of estival produce, dreaming of the days when I can eat veggies that aren't shipped from other parts of the country where it's *still* warm.

But summer in Baton Rouge means my dreams can be actualized—corn is abundant, and so are the ruby red sweet tomatoes you can find only in Louisiana. Whatever produce I want—fruit or vegetable—I've got it, and sweet yellow corn has quickly become a staple in my seasonal kitchen.

Granted, corn isn't a Louisiana good, but it seeps into our dishes like a close cousin. I suggest taking a step away from the normal tomatoes-only salsa and step toward summertime innovation: Black Bean Corn Salsa complete with a large helping of cilantro and red tomatoes. My recipe suggests 2 ears of fresh corn, but go ahead, live dangerously and add 3. After all, they're only 20¢ apiece!

3 very large tomatoes, chopped

1 cup cilantro, chopped fine

1 jalapeño, chopped fine (leave seeds for a spicier salsa)

¼ cup red onion, chopped fine

salt and pepper, to taste

¼ cup lime juice (about 2 small limes freshly juiced)

2 ears corn, steamed and removed from the cob

1 (15.5-ounce) can black beans, drained

Want to make this salsa even more savory? Add two large grilled Portobello mushroom caps (chopped) to the dip for a meaty natural flavor.

1   Prep ingredients: Chop washed tomatoes, cilantro, jalapeño, and red onion. Add to a mixing bowl.

2   Toss with salt, pepper, lime juice, corn, and black beans.

3   Season to taste and serve with tortilla chips. Makes 15 servings.

Fig and Prosciutto Salad
with Goat Cheese and Spinach

BEFORE I EMBRACE all that autumn has to offer (pumpkin, pears, apples, and gourds), I'm on a summer fresh fig kick. I can't help myself—figs are so beautiful, tasty, and go with anything. When I cut into a fig and see its bright red and yellow colors, I think, "Gosh, that would go good on . . ." and the list of tapas, salads, and desserts flood my brain.

In fact, readers of my blog Clearly Delicious have recognized my obsession with Louisiana figs. Everything from fig tarts to fig preserves to figs in oatmeal grace many previous posts. To them, I say, "See? Figs truly go well with or on anything!"

This recipe is a Brigman take on an antipasti classic. Ever since my last visit to Maine, I've been carrying around a cheap hardcopy cookbook titled "Antipasti." It cost $5, cannot be found anywhere, and has only about twenty recipes. The reason I bought the book? A version of this antipasti graced the cover. I had to have it! For buying fresh figs this fall, check your local farmers' market or produce stand. A list of resources (online and local) may be found in the back resources index.

As on the cover of my cheap hardcopy cookbook, I have prepared figs the way they should always be served—bedded at room temperature with classic Italian cured ham prosciutto and spinach greens. The dish offers homage to classic antipasti menus everywhere with an elegant simplicity sure to please the most fig-loving dinner guest.

5 figs, quartered

3 strips prosciutto, cut into slices

1 ounce goat cheese, broken into pieces

1 large handful spinach

1   Wash figs and spinach and prepare: Quarter figs, slice prosciutto, and break up goat cheese.

2   Plate salad: In a circular round, plate the prosciutto so that you have a border for your spinach. Fill in the center with a handful of fresh spinach and top with quartered figs and goat cheese. Serve with any light vinaigrette or infused balsamic vinegar. Makes 1 serving; double recipe for a lunch for two.

Summer Gazpacho
with Avocado and Cucumber

A DELICIOUS COLD summer soup with avocado and cucumber is both cooling and nutritious. Cold summer soups introduce any meal with the perfect blend of refreshing coolness and the natural flavors of summer produce like cucumbers, red peppers, and avocado. For this recipe, the avocado adds creaminess to the gazpacho as a way to counterbalance the watery nature of the cucumber.

1 avocado, cubed

1 cucumber, diced

1 small onion, chopped fine

6 large or 8 medium ripe tomatoes off the vine, seeds removed and peeled

2–3 cloves garlic, minced or pressed

1 cup roasted red peppers

salt and pepper, to taste

1 lime, quartered

DRESS GAZPACHO (BEFORE SERVING) WITH:

cucumbers, diced

onion, chopped fine

avocado, cubed

croutons

For cooking time, using store-bought jarred roasted red peppers will work great, but if you have the time to dedicate to roasting your own red peppers, see "Cooking Methods, Techniques, and Food Preservation" in the cooking primer of this book.

1 Cube avocado, dice cucumber, chop onion, and set aside.

2 Using a paring knife, score the bottom of your tomatoes with a large "X." Place tomatoes in an oversized bowl in your sink and cover with hot boiling water for 30 seconds to a minute. Immediately after exposing tomatoes to the hot water bath, drain using a colander and cover in ice. This last step is referred to as an "ice bath" and allows the skins to pull right off because of the drastic shift in temperature. Truthfully, there is no other way to peel tomatoes.

3 Peel tomatoes starting with the bottom score marks and remove seeds. Add to a food processor along with minced or pressed garlic, half of the cubed avocado, half of the diced cucumber, and half of the chopped onion. Reserve the remaining halves for dressing the gazpacho when serving. Pulse into a smooth mixture and season with salt and pepper to taste. Refrigerate gazpacho for at least an hour before serving.

4 When serving, dress gazpacho with the juice of a lime wedge, cucumbers, onion, avocado, and croutons. Makes 4 servings.

Crawfish Étouffée Ravioli
with Spicy Cream Sauce

SINCE MOVING TO Louisiana, I've been craving crawfish ravioli, but in none of the ways it's frequently served in our restaurants. Ravioli—a traditional Italian dish—beckons eaters to indulge in cheese, cream sauce, and many quintessential Italian herbs that really go great with crawfish-stuffed pasta dishes but just don't taste entirely Louisiana (not to me, anyway). I know many people feel the same way as I do: add crawfish to a dish and suddenly it's Louisiana cooking? Hardly this thinking can ever really be the case.

But, add a classic crawfish base—such as an étouffée—and now, we're talking a Louisiana fusion with classic Italian cooking.

My concept for these Crawfish Étouffée Raviolis is an effortless reinvention of a traditional étouffée: prepare étouffée with crawfish and enjoy only to reheat the leftovers the very next day. But instead of serving the same meal over rice, stuff pre-cooked lasagna sheets with pockets of étouffée filling. Ravioli filled with étouffée undoubtedly embodies Louisiana cooking, and your dining companion will be surprised that the dish is pasta instead of rice.

This recipe is designed to save time without sacrificing the gourmet nature of the dish. I suggest the use of pre-cooked lasagna sheets for speed and flavor, but for a fabulous homemade basic ravioli dough, see "Cooking Methods, Techniques, and Food Preservation" at the beginning of this book.

CRAWFISH ÉTOUFFÉE FILLING

1 onion, chopped fine

1 celery stick, chopped fine

1–2 tablespoons fresh parsley, chopped fine

2 green onions, chopped fine

½ green bell pepper, chopped

½ red bell pepper, chopped

1–2 tablespoons ground chili powder, to taste

1 stick salted butter, room temperature

1 pound crawfish tails

1½ cups water

2 cloves garlic, minced or pressed

3–4 bay leaves

salt and pepper, to taste

cayenne, to taste

1 tablespoon flour

PASTA

1 box lasagna sheets OR pasta recipe in the "Cooking Methods, Techniques, and Food Preparation" section.

flour, for dusting surface

1 egg, beaten

For easy instructions on how to make your own chili powder, see the Introduction of this book.

1   Prepare filling for ravioli as you would a traditional étouffée: Chop ingredients—onion, celery, green onions, parsley, and peppers. Set aside. Pulse dried chili into a powder following the directions in "Stocking Your Pantry" at beginning of this book (skip this step if using store-bought chili powder or cayenne).

2   In a large nonstick skillet, melt butter over medium-high heat and sauté chopped vegetables for 10 minutes, or until tender. Add crawfish tails, ½ cup water, minced or pressed garlic, and spices—homemade chili powder and bay leaves. Reduce heat to medium, cover and cook for an additional 10 minutes, making sure to stir occasionally.

3   Slowly add in 1 tablespoon flour and 1 cup water in divided increments: First, sprinkle mixture with half a tablespoon of flour, mix, ½ cup water, mix, and the remaining half of the flour and water. Allow mixture to cook uncovered for about 3–5 minutes or until the étouffée has thickened. Taste and season with salt, pepper, and parsley. Remove étouffée from heat and serve.

4   Prepare ravioli shells: Cook one box lasagna sheets according to package instructions, remove from heat, and allow pasta to set in water while preparing ravioli pieces (draining the pasta forces it to lose moisture quickly, though it will still be sticky when filling with the étouffée. Fortunately, the next two steps are fairly quick, so you won't have to worry about overcooking the pasta).

SPICY CREAM SAUCE

1 pint heavy cream

1 stick salted butter, softened

½ cup Parmesan, freshly grated, more for sprinkling plates

1 (14.5-ounce) can roasted red tomatoes, drained

1 teaspoon chili powder

salt and pepper, to taste

5   Stuff ravioli and prepare: On a well-floured surface, place one sheet cooked lasagna that has been lightly patted dry with a paper towel. Dollop teaspoons of the étouffée mixture 1–2 inches apart down the strip of lasagna. Brush edges with beaten egg and between each dollop. Top with another sheet of cooked lasagna that has also been patted dry.

6   Between each dollop, press the lasagna sheets onto themselves to seal out air and form distinctive raviolis using a ravioli press or overturned glass.

7   Plate ravioli immediately after pressing out and sprinkle with Parmesan, parsley, and salt and pepper.

8   Prepare Spicy Cream Sauce: In a nonstick pan, heat heavy cream over low-medium heat adding 1 tablespoon butter at a time, whisking to combine mixture as the butter melts. Stir in Parmesan cheese, roasted red tomatoes, chili powder, and salt and pepper to taste. Allow sauce to cook for 5 minutes or until flavors are blended. Serve over Crawfish Étouffée Ravioli and top with grated Parmesan cheese. Makes 4–6 servings.

If at any point the étouffée appears to be too thick, use sparing amounts of the extra cup of water to add moisture to the sauce.

Fig and Prosciutto Pizza with Brie,
and Boudin Pizza

ONE OF THE best gifts I've ever received was a simple $10 pizza stone from one of my best friends. Although a baking sheet will do for any pizza, pizza stones should be placed in the oven and warmed to piping hot before baking your pie on it. This simple device helps create restaurant-style flavor with very little work and all because you're using a stone instead of metal.

In the summer, I look for any reason to cook outside, in part because I like to keep my house cool but also because a grill is a wonderful device that need not be wasted. Just as a pizza stone enhances the flavor of a homemade pie, a grill adds similar smoky-summer flavor to your crust and toppings. Combine this base with sweet figs and salty prosciutto for a pizza with such a beautiful combination of salty and sweet, it'll dazzle any dinner guest.

Special equipment needed/suggested: grill, pizza stone, mezzaluna or pizza knife (see description in the Kitchen Tools/Equipment List).

1 serving pizza dough (see recipe in "Cooking Methods, Techniques and Food Preservation")

1–2 cups homemade tomato sauce (can substitute with supermarket variety)

1 cup mozzarella cheese, cubed

1 (8-ounce) Brie wheel, rind removed and cubed

2 cups figs, halved

2–4 ounces prosciutto, thinly sliced

salt and pepper, to taste

1   Prepare dough: Preheat oven to 375F and place pizza stone in the center of oven for 30 minutes. On a clean, well-floured surface, roll out pre-made pizza dough into a circular round. Transfer to a pre-heated pizza stone that has been sprinkled with cornmeal once out of the oven.

2   Drizzle 1–2 tablespoons olive oil on dough and brush to coat. Using a fork, evenly pierce the dough all over.

3   Dress pizza: Spread 1–2 cups red tomato sauce on pizza, season with salt, pepper, and Italian herbs such as thyme, rosemary, and parsley, top with spinach, mozzarella, brie, and the last of your seasonings (again with salt, pepper, and Italian herbs). Halve figs, thinly slice prosciutto, and spread across pizza surface. Drizzle pizza lightly with olive oil.

Italian herbs, to taste (I suggest thyme, rosemary, and parsley)

cornmeal, for dough ball

flour, for rolling

4   Baking pizza: Bake at 375F for 25–35 minutes, or until crust is done and cheese is golden brown. Remove pizza from oven and allow to rest for five minutes before cutting.

OR

Grilling pizza: Transfer pie from a nonheated pizza stone to a hot grill that has been brushed in cooking oil. Cover and grill pizza for as little as 5–7 minutes or as long as 10–12 minutes until the bottom is golden brown, the cheese has melted, and the dough is cooked all the way through.

5   Remove pizza from grill and rest for five minutes. Cut into slices using a pizza cutter or a mezzaluna and serve. Makes 4 servings.

BOUDIN PIZZA ALTERNATIVE

1   Follow above directions, but substitute for prosciutto blackened or white Boudin.

Grilled Sausage Bedded with
Blackened Summer Squash

IN 2011, I participated in a recipe challenge with a company called Marx Foods—a specialty food and meats distributor that has traditionally supplied four- and five-star kitchens with high-quality and exotic ingredients. My winning recipe for "Chocolate Azteca Cupcakes" received the most incredible award any food writer could possibly imagine: sausage. Not just any sausage: $150 worth of the meat ranging from buffalo, to duck, to venison, to wild boar. Regular versions with chicken and pork with red wine were included as well, but a new experience awaited me in wild game and other exotic ingredients. This simple grilled sausage with summer squash is one of my favorite recipes from that time.

Grilled Sausage Bedded with Blackened Summer Squash goes wonderfully as a side dish or entrée with my Fig and Prosciutto Pizza with Brie listed in this section, but will also excite guests at a summer crawfish boil or even at a potluck tailgating party.

Grilling baskets work wonders when cooking with vegetables outside. If you don't have a grilling basket, substitute regular cooking spears or an aluminum foil basket.

1 pound zucchini, sliced

1 pound yellow summer squash, sliced

1–2 tablespoons infused olive oil, such as the Basil-Infusion from Vom Fass New Orleans

1 tablespoon infused olive oil, such as the Cayenne-Infusion from Vom Fass New Orleans

salt and pepper, to taste

A Word on Olive Oil Selection: two infused variations of extra virgin olive oil are suggested for this recipe because of the flavor they add either to the meat or vegetables. Although such options make for a wonderful cooking experience if you have them, regular extra virgin olive oil works great here as well. For preparing your own infusions, see "Cooking Methods, Techniques, and Preservation" at the beginning of this book.

1 tablespoon parsley, chopped fine

2 tablespoons basil, chopped fine

1 pound sausage (any store-bought sausage based on taste preference)

1   Prepare summer squash: Wash and slice zucchini and yellow summer squash into circular rounds. Place in large bowl and toss with basil-infused olive oil and salt and pepper to taste. Place inside grilling basket and grill covered for 15–20 minutes flipping regularly until squash is tender. Remove from heat and cool. Chop parsley and basil.

2   Prepare sausage: Lightly brush with spicy olive oil (if you have it), then grill alongside squash for 15–20 minutes, or until both sides are blackened and cooked all the way through. Remove from heat and allow to rest for several minutes before cutting into circular pieces.

3   Plate squash with sausage on top. Sprinkle with chopped parsley, basil, and a little cracked pepper and coarse salt and serve. Makes 4–6 servings.

Spicy Shrimp Cocktail

IN THE EARLY DAYS of Clearly Delicious, I made sure to test my favorite Louisiana staples, with shrimp cocktail being the very first one. A go-to-favorite in my kitchen, shrimp cocktail wows guests more than ever when served with a good-quality spicy dipping sauce. Whipped together in seconds from everyday sauces—Tabasco, ketchup, horseradish, and chili sauce, this dip is much more complex than any of the store-bought "cocktail sauce" sold in glass jars. Simultaneously sweet and spicy, homemade cocktail sauce makes for a perfect appetizer or decadent entrée on any hot Louisiana summer day. Serve alongside Gulf shrimp and you have the perfect summer treat that tastes like Louisiana albeit with some fresher ingredients of garlic and lemon.

SHRIMP

2 tablespoons Old Bay Seasoning

1 lemon, halved

2 cloves garlic, minced or pressed

1 teaspoon salt

½ teaspoon chili powder

1 pound extra large shrimp, peeled with tails intact

COCKTAIL SAUCE

½ cup chili sauce

1 cup ketchup

1 tablespoon horseradish

1 dash Worcestershire sauce

½ lemon, juiced

1 teaspoon Tabasco

1 clove garlic, minced or pressed

1   Bring a large pot of water to a boil with the Old Bay, lemon, garlic, and salt. Add shrimp to water fully peeled but with tails still on. Boil shrimp until brightly pink and drain (do not overcook).

2   While shrimp are cooling, combine chili sauce, ketchup, horseradish, Worcestershire, lemon, Tabasco, and garlic in a bowl, mixing until fully combined.

3   Plate shrimp with cocktail sauce and serve freshly boiled or chilled. Makes 2–4 servings.

Sirloin Steak with Herb Butter and (possibly) Egg

I'VE BEEN OVERSALTING my steaks for years because—unbeknownst to me—something magical happens during this preparatory process. Not being a chemist, I refer to this magic as purely "yummy," but food scientists will tell you there is a tenderizing method to salting meat before cooking: extra salt breaks down proteins and releases natural juices. The use of kosher salt suggested below truly yields the most succulent steak all because of this kitchen chemistry.

Restaurant-quality tenderness—and flavor—is possible for any steak by simply following this simple step: salt steak according to the ratio I outline in the instructions (basically, how thick your steak is determines how long you let it be exposed to large quantities of salt). For those worried about consuming too much salt, do not stress, as you will be washing this tenderizing agent off the steak before cooking, so see step 2.

Instead of dousing your summer dish with store-bought barbeque sauce this summer, serve steaks with dollops of herb butter for a sinfully good treat. Herb butter goes wonderfully on just about everything, so if you're worried that using it for an avant-garde steak recipe means you'll never use it again, then I encourage you to think about just how much we use butter for: herb butter with potatoes, herb butter with grilled corn, herb butter with bread, and yes, of course, herb butter with steak. You'll never eat a steak without a little herb butter again . . . now, the suggested cracked egg at the recipe's end may be an acquired taste.

any size cut of steak: sirloin, rib eye, or porterhouse

coarse salt such as kosher or sea, to coat

1 Prepare steak for tenderizing: Based on the thickness of your steak, you want to season it with salt for every inch of thickness. For example, a steak that's 1-inch thick requires one hour of tenderizing with salt; a steak that's 1½ inches thick requires an hour and a half of tenderizing, and so on and so forth. Cover steak on both sides with a thick layer of coarse salt such as sea or kosher. Leave steak out at

HERB RUB

2 tablespoons rosemary, chopped
fine

2 tablespoons parsley, chopped fine

2 tablespoons thyme, chopped fine

pepper, to taste

HERB BUTTER

1 stick salted butter, room
temperature

1 tablespoon parsley, chopped fine

1 tablespoon basil, chopped fine

1 tablespoon rosemary, chopped
fine

1 tablespoon thyme, chopped fine

1 clove garlic, minced or pressed

½ teaspoon pepper

room temperature covered and watch as the steak's natural juices increasingly rise to the skin as it tenderizes before your eyes. Salt is a natural tenderizer making the steak juicier as it breaks down the meat's proteins and enhances meat texture.

2   After steaks have tenderized, rinse with water thoroughly to remove excess salt. Salt adds wonderful flavor to any dish, but we're truly using it for its chemical properties at this point. Pat steaks dry to remove extra moisture from skin.

3   Season steak with a simple herb rub or pepper (*no* salt) and grill, broil, or pan fry on both sides based on desired doneness of steak. For tips on how to test steak's doneness, see "Cooking Methods, Techniques, and Food Preservation" for useful testing information.

4   Right before removing steak from grill, broiler, or other cooking surface, dollop pre-made herb butter on top so that the butter begins to melt. Makes anywhere from 1–4 servings based on steak size.

Optional: **Crack an egg on top and cook for 1–3 minutes (again, desired doneness here) for an afternoon variation of steak and eggs and serve.**

5   Prepare Herb Butter: In a large bowl, add softened butter, herbs, garlic, and pepper. Using a large spoon, mix to integrate until additions are fully incorporated into butter. Using a flat spatula, scrape butter mixture onto wax paper. Fold wax paper over mixture to cover fully and shape as you like—a long tube of butter or a brick of butter. Refrigerate butter until ready to use. Makes 8 tablespoons butter.

SIDE DISHES

Perfect Guacamole

AVOCADOS ARE GORGEOUS: dark green shells with cool mint green centers. Shaped like pears that have had a little too much to drink, avocados are an attractive fruit, but even more gorgeous on the inside.

Beautiful and clearly delicious. avocados grown from a specific California variety are notorious for having a more nut-like flavor, whereas avocados grown in Mexico are notoriously "blander" as they frequently take the "sting" out of spicy dishes. Whatever the case, Haas avocados are my favorite not only because they're a beautiful ripe summer fruit, but because they also taste incredible when mixed with jalapeño, tomato, onion, and cilantro. The result? A perfect guacamole.

My friend James has had many experiences working on an avocado farm in California and although I value his cooking skills immensely, he has a tendency of getting up on an avocado-connoisseur soapbox whenever he sees this recipe. My addition of fruit juice lacks a traditional feel and is "absolute rubbish," as he says in his Irish accent. If you've ever argued with an avocado connoisseur and an Irishman, you know that they can be quite convincing. For a variation with summertime brightness, add tablespoons of citrus juice as suggested here, but for a classic variation, skip this alternative. I hope James would be proud that I suggest his less-citrus-inspired version of making guacamole here as well!

Next time you're at the market this summer, make sure to take a moment to look at the avocados and you'll see exactly the beauty to which I'm referring. Avocados really are an attractive fruit. But don't stare too long, because you'll inevitably be tempted to take them home and eat.

¼ cup tomatoes, chopped

3 tablespoons fresh cilantro, chopped

1 jalapeño, chopped fine

2 tablespoons onion, minced

4 ripe Haas avocados, halved with pits removed

salt and pepper, to taste

2–3 tablespoons fresh lemon or lime juice

1 teaspoon jalapeño seeds, plus more to taste

1 Prepare your ingredients: Chop tomatoes, cilantro, and jalapeño. Mince onion and cut avocados in half.

2 Remove avocado pits (discard) and scoop avocado into a mortar and pestle. I use an oversized one that comes in handy for many food preparations.

3 Add cilantro, tomatoes, and jalapeño to the avocados and proceed to mash until smooth. Season with salt, pepper, cilantro, lemon/lime juice, and jalapeño seeds to taste. I know my guacamole is done when it has a sense of "heat" in the aftertaste, but still strikes me as somewhat salty and earthy on the first bite. Serve with tortilla chips and enjoy! Makes 6 servings.

For other uses for a kitchen mortar and pestle, see my "Kitchen Tools and Equipment List" at the beginning of this book.

Blistered Eggplant with Mozzarella

DURING THE SUMMER months, I can't get enough of eggplant—grilled, blackened, or blistered. There's nothing I like more than experimenting with eggplant. Many southern Louisianans eat eggplant in its commercial forms—Eggplant Parmesan anyone?—but the purple summer fruit makes for a wonderful side dish, entrée, and yes, even appetizer.

Roast on your summer grill, broil in your oven, or blister on your stovetop for an easy vegetarian-friendly dish. Whenever I have a dinner guest who doesn't eat meat, I always make sure to have several side dish options to play center stage as the main meal. This blistered eggplant with the addition of melted mozzarella feels as hardy as any meat dish and, in my mind, even more flavorful.

Whether you're a meat-eating carnivore or a dedicated vegetarian, try blistering fresh garden eggplant with melted mozzarella at your next summer gathering.

1 cup mozzarella, cubed very small

2–3 green onions, chopped

2 tablespoons basil, chopped fine

1 tablespoon Italian parsley leaves, whole

2 tablespoons olive oil, plus more for dressing

2 tablespoons red wine vinegar

2 pounds eggplant, cut into 1-inch-thick circular slices

salt and pepper, to taste

1   Cube mozzarella and chop green onions and basil. De-stem Italian parsley leaves. Toss mozzarella, onions, and herbs in olive oil and red wine vinegar. Set aside.

2   Wash eggplant, remove stems, and cut into circular rounds. Line across an olive oil brushed baking sheet and sprinkle with salt, pepper, and more olive oil.

3   For grilling: Place seasoned eggplant in grilling basket and grill (closed) for 10–15 minutes or until eggplant is lightly blackened ("blistered") on both sides. Plate grilled eggplant and dress with cheese and spice mixture. Crack fresh pepper over blistered eggplant.

OR

For broiling: When it's necessary to skip the grill, heat oven broiler to high and place eggplant directly underneath. Broil for 6–8 minutes or until "blistered" and flip, doing the same for the other side. Oven times may vary. Plate broiled eggplant and dress with cheese and herb mixture and top with cracked fresh pepper and serve. Makes 8–10 servings.

Smoked Salmon Carpaccio with Dill, Capers, and Quail Eggs

MINIMALIST COOKING TECHNIQUES speak best to my mood in warm summer months—I want everything light, fresh, and quickly plated so I can kick up my feet and return to my summer books. In this vein, I often skip smoking my own meats for pre-smoked versions I can pick up at our local markets. My preference? Smoked salmon, as it's deeply flavorful and easy to cut carpaccio-style. Plate with a great herb like dill, some exotic hard-boiled quail eggs, and capers and let the subtle lavishness of smoked fish feed your summer belly.

The term "carpaccio"—as fancy as it sounds—refers simply to how thinly a dish is cut. Reserved for smoked meats and fishes, carpaccio dishes can be cut thinly and then pounded to tenderize (most often with beefs and other smoked meats). For this easy and light carpaccio, I suggest cutting the smoked salmon as thinly as possible, but you can easily substitute smoked meats such as beef tenderloin if you're not a huge fan of salmon.

12 ounces smoked salmon, cut as thinly as possible ("carpaccio")

2 tablespoons dill, chopped fine

1 teaspoon pepper, plus more to taste

1 cup arugula, packed

2 tablespoons capers

4 quail eggs, halved (can substitute regular boiled eggs)

salt, to taste

1   Rub smoked salmon in dill and pepper all over. Cut salmon as thinly as possible ("carpaccio" style) and plate on bed of washed arugula.

2   Dress sliced salmon with capers and halved quail eggs. Crack additional fresh pepper and a few pinches of salt over the dish and serve. Makes 4 servings.

Corn Bread "Soufflé"

MY GRANDMOTHER USED to make a corn soufflé using classic nuclear family ingredients: canned corn, canned milk, and saltine crackers. Although delicious in its ode to industrial and modern ingredients, the dish certainly wasn't the epitome of "freshness." As a Louisiana resident, I've grown to love the extraordinary amounts of corn everywhere starting in June and the endless ways to use it as suggested in my Black Bean Corn Salsa recipe at the beginning of this section. For a way to incorporate freshness into side bakery items, substitute fresh whole corn in muffins, corn bread, and even "soufflés." Don't let grandma's recipe title fool you, as there's nothing French or complicated in these cooking techniques at all—simply stir and bake. Whether it's a "soufflé" may be debatable, but whether it's fresh certainly will not.

Inspired by my grandmother's Thanksgiving classic, this recipe incorporates fresh summer corn to an otherwise 1950s casserole dish. I use fresh summer corn here, but this dish can be made any month of the year with canned corn.

1½ cups self-rising cornmeal

¾ cup sugar

½ teaspoon baking soda

pinch of salt

1 cup grated cheddar cheese

2 eggs

1 cup whole milk

2 ears corn, cooked and de-cobbed

Using self-rising cornmeal is paramount here so that the soufflé actually puffs up and has texture. To add your own leavening to a cornmeal that isn't self-rising, simply use 1 tablespoon baking powder and ½ teaspoon salt for every 1 cup cornmeal.

1   Preheat oven to 350F. Combine dry ingredients—cornmeal, sugar, baking soda, and salt—with cheddar cheese. Mix together milk and two cracked eggs into the dry mixture and fold into fresh corn.

2   Pour batter into a greased casserole dish or cast-iron skillet and bake for 40–50 minutes, or until corn soufflé is golden brown and a toothpick comes out clean. Serve and enjoy! Makes 6–8 servings.

I like to grease casserole dishes with bacon grease if I have it. The subtle bacon flavor never fails to wow guests at breakfast, lunch, or dinner.

Pasta Salad with Zucchini, Almonds, and Goat Cheese

IT'S IMPOSSIBLE TO attend a summer barbeque in Louisiana without a pasta salad. Summer just isn't summer without a go-to chilled pasta salad recipe to serve to lunch and dinner guests. For me, I avoid almost anything that involves ranch, but have found a fabulous substitute for our favorite American pasta salad ingredient—goat cheese. The semisoft texture holds nicely to everything from spiral pasta ("fusilli") to elbow. As for taste, the tart yet creamy flavor offers a refreshing bite to any summer palette.

Part of the summertime sophistication in this dish comes directly from the use of goat cheese. Not a fan of the tangy ingredient? Substitute a milder ricotta or more Parmesan to please your palette. Special equipment needed: standard kitchen grater (see my "Kitchen Tools and Equipment List" at the beginning of this book).

½–1 pound pasta

½ cup slivered almonds, toasted and cooled

2 zucchinis (about 1 to 1½ pounds) halved lengthwise and cut very thinly ("carpaccio style")

1 teaspoon salt

1 cup Parmesan

1 cup semisoft goat cheese

freshly ground black pepper, to taste

5 tablespoons olive oil (I use equal parts regular olive oil and Walnut-Infused Olive Oil from Fioré)

juice of a lemon

1   Bring a large pot of salted water to a boil. Before prepping your pot, spray the pot's bottom with a thick coat of nonstick spray, then add your water and salt. This step will ensure that very little pasta sticks to the bottom (and guess what? It works!). As I always suggest, follow the Italian cooking tip for good pasta water: pasta water should taste like the ocean (within reason, of course).

2   Add pasta to pot when boiling and cook until al dente—tender, but still firm—and strain, allowing to rest and cool 5 minutes (remember to keep tossing your pasta so that it doesn't begin to stick together as it dries).

3   Toast almonds lightly for several minutes in a small skillet with nonstick spray over medium-low heat. Remove from heat and cool.

4   Wash zucchini, de-stem, and cut in half lengthwise. Using the flat side-slot on a standard kitchen grater, thinly slice your zucchini. Zucchini should be very thin, carpaccio-style. Add zucchini to a colander and salt thoroughly. Allow zucchini to rest and drain for 20 minutes.

5 Transfer zucchini to a bowl and add toasted almonds, Parmesan, goat cheese, and pepper. Toss to combine.

6 Prepare marinade: Add 2½ tablespoons regular olive oil with 2½ tablespoons walnut-infused olive oil. Whisk together with the juice of one lemon. Add drained pasta to marinade with tossed zucchini mixture and combine all ingredients. Taste and adjust with salt and pepper as necessary and serve. Makes 8–10 servings.

See my "Kitchen Tools and Equipment List" for a full explanation of how to accomplish "carpaccio"-style cutting with the use of a standard kitchen grater.

DESSERTS

Fruit Salad with Blood Orange Olive Oil and
Blueberry Balsamic Dressing

I KNOW THAT summer is getting closer when the fruit begins to outnumber the vegetables at my local produce market. Bins filled with large cantaloupes, containers stuffed with oversized blueberries, and ripe vibrant strawberries stare at me as I walk down the aisles. I'm desperately looking for arugula, but all I can see are gorgeous fruits begging me to take them home. So, I do.

If I were to list the top five dishes I eat on a regular basis, fresh fruit would fight for the number one spot every time (next to embellished salads with figs and balsamic vinegars).

But my favorite trick is a simple, vibrant fruit salad coated in a light, summery vinaigrette that can be made right at home. I've known many of my friends to serve fruit salads with a whipped cream glaze, covering the natural colors of the fruit with manufactured sugar, thus masking the actual ingredients. These fruit salads are always good, but I favor presentation and freshness over more sugary options. Recently, I tried an amazing homemade vinaigrette—blood orange olive oil and blueberry balsamic vinegar—and coated my fruit in this concoction. I could not have been happier with the rich, fresh fruit and the subtle hints of blood orange and blueberry as my guests and I ate it.

This recipe is a standard fruit salad and can be made a variety of ways. I prefer cantaloupe, pineapple, strawberries, and fresh blueberries or blackberries. Some people add bananas to their fruit salad, but I find them to be a bit of a hassle (not only do they mash when mixing your fruit, but they also have very high oxidation indicators where they brown once exposed to the air). If you do choose to use bananas in this recipe, cut them up right before serving to avoid the trouble of browning fruit.

A word on vinaigrette: if you don't have infused olive oils or balsamic vinegar immediately at your disposal, substitute regular extra virgin olive oil and balsamic vinegar with the addition of an orange, juiced.

1 pineapple, cored and cubed

1 cantaloupe, seeded and cubed

1½ cups strawberries, de-stemmed and quartered

1 cup blueberries

1 cup green or red grapes

2–3 tablespoons blood orange olive oil, like the one from Fioré

2–3 tablespoons blueberry balsamic vinegar, like the one from Fioré

1 Begin by prepping your fruit: Core and cube pineapple, seed and cube cantaloupe, de-stem and quarter strawberries, and wash blueberries.

2 Add fruit to a large mixing bowl and toss lightly to combine.

3 In a separate, smaller bowl, add balsamic vinegar and olive oil. Whisk to combine and pour over fruit mixture. Toss fruit mixture lightly and transfer to serving bowl. Serve fruit by itself or with whipped cream or crème fraîche. Makes 8 servings.

Because of the natural darkness of balsamic vinegar, you will see a certain darkened sheen over some of your fruit. In fact, it may stain lighter fruits like the cantaloupe and pineapple. This result is to be expected, and the salad still tastes excellent.

Raspberry Almond Cream Cheese Tartlets

EVER TRY TO make homemade cheesecake? It's a pain, and so much can go wrong—the cheesecake "cracks," it doesn't set right, and heaven forbid you use the wrong pan!

Well, I've long ago come up with a solution for those of us who are "Cheesecake Challenged"—cheesecakes prepared on a smaller scale with sweet fruity syrups to hide any imperfections. My Raspberry Almond Cream Cheese Tartlets dressed in strawberry puree and ripe raspberries taste just like cheesecake (and in fact, are made the same way), but on a smaller scale for individual portions. Plus, they're pretty low fat too.

Made with fresh raspberries, homemade strawberry puree, easy, yummy graham cracker crust, these tartlets serve six quantities of clearly delicious fruity, creamy, and almond flavor.

Special equipment needed/suggested: 10½ x 10 tartlets pan.

CRUST

8 sheets graham crackers (16 crackers), broken up and crumbled

3–4 teaspoons water

1 tablespoon vanilla extract

2 tablespoons sugar

2 tablespoons butter, melted

1   Preheat oven to 350F. Prepare the crust: Process broken-up graham crackers in food processor until they are crumbs.

2   Add water, vanilla extract, sugar, and melted butter. Pulse to combine (you'll know it's done when the crust mixture has begun to stick to the sides of the processor).

3   Spoon 3 tablespoons (maybe more, maybe less) graham cracker crumbs into the tartlet shells. Press down with a tablespoon, making sure that the bottom is properly lined and the sides also (it's key to have a graham cracker crust siding as this texture is what allows the tart to leave the baking shell properly.

4   Bake for 10 minutes at 350F, or until crust is golden brown. Remove from oven and cool.

FILLING

1 (8-ounce) package regular cream cheese (can use low fat)

¼ cup sugar (can use less for a tarter cheesecake)

1 teaspoon vanilla extract

1 teaspoon almond extract

1 teaspoon finely grated lemon zest

TOPPING

2 cups strawberries, pureed

⅓–½ cup sugar, to taste

1 tablespoon fresh lemon juice

1 tablespoon cornstarch

1 pint-size basket raspberries

3 tablespoons sliced almonds

5   Prepare the cream cheese filling: In a standing mixer, mix cream cheese with sugar, extracts, and lemon zest. Spread mixture evenly over cooled tartlet crusts.

6   Prepare the fruit glaze: Quarter strawberries and process until pureed. Add strawberries, sugar, lemon juice, and cornstarch to a small skillet. Warm over medium-high heat until simmering. Simmer strawberry mixture for one minute, continually whisking. Remove from heat and cool.

7   Spoon puree over tartlets and smooth it. Wash raspberries and arrange over the tartlets. Sprinkle with almonds along the sides of the tart's outer edge. Refrigerate for 2–3 hours before serving or removing from tartlet shell. The tartlets keep well overnight, but make sure to cover. Makes 6 servings.

Blueberry Balsamic Gelato

THERE'S SOMETHING SO insanely easy about making your own gelato. For years, I told Clearly Delicious readers that I refused to post gelato recipes for the fear that I'd be making ice creams and frozen yogurts every week. But during summer months, there must be an exception. Served at the end of a hot summer day, gelato offers an impressive finishing touch that cleans post-meal palette. To make the dish even more elegant, garnish with fresh blueberries on top.

This recipe reminds me of the Blueberry Balsamico you can sometimes find at La Divina Gelateria on Magazine Street in New Orleans. Their version joins blueberries with regular sweet and tart balsamic vinegar in a combination that dazzles a thirsty summer palette. For a homemade tribute to a New Orleans favorite, try a blueberry-infused balsamic vinegar for extra sweetness and flavor. Don't have blueberry balsamic vinegar? Use the regular variety, or try any of the other optional ingredient variations listed below—lemon, lime, or lavender.

But blueberries are my favorite ingredient—nature's power fruit, blueberries are filled with antioxidants, fiber, and Vitamin C; this is one ice cream that just might help make a beautiful body. So eat up. This Blueberry Balsamic Gelato invites the quintessential flavors of summer with the health of nature's most powerful fruit.

Special equipment needed: Cuisinart Ice Cream Maker, or like device; see my "Kitchen Tools and Equipment List" at the beginning of this book for ice cream maker suggestions.

3 cups blueberries

¼ cup jam (blueberry if you have it)

¼ cup water

pinch of salt

3 large egg yolks

¾–1 cup sugar, based on taste

2 cups whole milk

3 tablespoons balsamic vinegar (blueberry balsamic vinegar like the one from Fioré if you have it)

1   Combine blueberries, jam, water, and salt in a medium-large non-stick saucepan and bring to a boil. Reduce heat to medium and simmer for 8 to 10 minutes, or until mixture has thickened considerably.

2   Cool mixture lightly and blend until smooth in a food processor. Set aside.

3   In a standing mixer, beat egg yolks into sugar until thick and sticky. Warm milk over medium-high heat in a saucepan similar to the one in step 1 until just before boiling. Add one half of hot milk to sugar and yolks and whisk to combine. Add last half of hot milk and continue whisking until fully integrated.

4   Transfer to a saucepan similar to the one used in step 1 and warm on medium-low heat until the mixture coats the back of a spoon (anywhere from 4 to 8 minutes). Remove from heat and bring to room temperature.

5   Whisking slowly, stir blueberry blend into dairy blend. Add balsamic vinegar or seasoning option—lemon, lavender, lime, etc. Pour into basin of an ice cream maker and freeze according to machine's instruction manual. Serve when gelato is fully frozen. Makes 4 servings.

Optional Variations: **For those who do not have the same adoration for balsamic vinegars as I do, you might consider substituting for this ingredient any of these variations: 3 tablespoons lemon juice, 3 tablespoons lime juice, or 3 tablespoons lavender, ground to a powder.**

Key Lime Cheesecake Tarts

KEY LIME AND I do not have the best of histories. Upon hearing that a good friend liked key lime pie, I went out of my way to make her a homemade variation. The result? A pie containing disastrous cracks and a questionable crust. I have since attempted dozens of variations of this staple southern dessert item and finally settled on the fact that this pie and I still have some issues to work out. Cheesecake in the form of bite-size bars may just be the answer.

Although the main ingredient in these tarts is different from my Raspberry Almond Cream Cheese Tartlets, these Key Lime Cheesecake Tarts are a notably delicious relative. The key is to use actual key limes—not regular limes—for their distinct tart flavor. The variation may seem subtle, but the final result is powerfully delicious.

So try these easy, brightly colored green cheesecake tarts for an indulgent afternoon snack, over cocktails with friends, or for dessert.

CRUST

8 sheets graham crackers (16 crackers), broken up and crumbled

3–4 teaspoons water

1 teaspoon vanilla extract

1 teaspoon almond extract

2 tablespoons sugar

2 tablespoons butter, melted

1 Preheat oven to 350F.

2 Prepare graham cracker crust: Process graham cracker pieces in food processor until crumbs. Add water, vanilla and almond extract, sugar, and melted butter. Pulse to combine (you'll know it's done when the crust mixture has begun to stick to the sides of the processor).

3 Spray tart shells with baking spray and spoon 3 tablespoons (maybe more, maybe less) graham cracker crumbs into the shells. Press down with a tablespoon, making sure that the bottom is properly lined and so are the sides—it's key to have a graham cracker crust siding as this texture is what allows the tart to leave the baking shell properly.

4 Bake for 10 minutes at 350F, or until crust is golden brown. Remove from oven and cool crusts.

KEY LIME FILLING

¾ cup sugar

2 (8-ounce) packages regular cream cheese, softened

2 cups plain Greek yogurt

3 eggs + 1 large egg white

2 key limes, juiced (a little less than ½ cup juice)

1 key lime, zested

½ cup regular sour cream

green food coloring

yellow food coloring

5   Prepare the cream cheese filling: In a standing mixer, beat sugar and cream cheese until smooth; add yogurt, eggs and extra egg white, lime juice, and all but 1 tablespoon zest into cream cheese and sugar mixture. Beat until smooth and blended.

6   Separate cream cheese filling in half. Pour one half of cream cheese filling into the 6 graham cracker crusts so that the shells are only just about halfway full.

7   Using the remaining cream cheese filling, color with any combination of green and yellow food coloring until cream cheese is a desired bright green color. I love the natural neon shades of key limes, so I try to match the color of the green cream cheese with the limes I recently used. Once this is colored, you're ready to combine the colored cream cheese with the regular white cream cheese.

8   Dollop 1 or 2 tablespoons green cream cheese filling on top of the half-filled cheesecake shells. Using a toothpick, swirl green cream cheese mixture into the regular cream cheese, creating any pattern that you like (I prefer a marbling pattern, which is easily accomplished with the aid of a toothpick).

9   Bake cream cheese tarts in oven for 15 minutes or until cheesecake has set. Remove from oven and cool. Dress in remaining lime zest, serve, and enjoy! Makes 6 tarts.

Banana Pudding

ONE OF MY first jobs cooking professionally was a not-so-glamorous position doing food prep for dessert items in the kitchen of a major chain restaurant. The jobs in rural South Carolina were limited and if I wanted to buy a sparkly prom dress, well, I had to work in a kitchen during high school. For me, this work was with banana pudding.

I came to love banana pudding in those early days where "professional" cooking was completely new to me. The ingredients were simple and easy, and I never seemed to get the recipe wrong. Customers on Sunday would always approach me asking to bring out another pan of their favorite southern dessert and they'd spoon large bowls full of the banana-filled vanilla pudding and dress it with "Nilla" wafers.

Since I love southern staples that can be dressed up or down, I suggest a more sophisticated variation of the classic I made as a teenager. Instead of using store-bought pudding, prepare an easy homemade custard that adds a certain flavorful "wow" factor to the classic use of vanilla wafers and freshly cubed bananas.

This recipe takes a cue from the custard used in my Tarte aux Baies in the spring desserts section, but with a banana infusion. Trying to save time? Use high-quality store-bought vanilla pudding for this recipe, but one taste of this homemade custard and I'm thinking you'll always find the time.

CUSTARD

8 egg yolks

1 cup granulated sugar

6 tablespoons cornstarch

4 cups whole milk (skim milk works fine)

½ cup (1 stick) unsalted butter

2 teaspoons vanilla extract

2 teaspoons almond extract

4 bananas, sliced

Optional: substitute Biscoff cookies for half of the vanilla wafers.

1   Prepare the custard/filling: Whisk together egg yolks, half of the sugar, and cornstarch.

2   In a large, nonstick saucepan, whisk the remaining half of the sugar with 4 cups milk and bring to a boil, stirring occasionally.

3   Once milk and sugar mixture is boiling, pour ¼ of the milk mixture

TOPPINGS

2 bananas, sliced

1 box vanilla ("Nilla") wafers

whipped cream

into your reserved whisked egg mixture to "temper" the wet ingredients, stirring constantly while you do this step. Remove milk mixture from heat and slowly add the egg mixture into the milk mixture in the heated saucepan. Return this wet mixture to medium-high heat and whisk until the cream thickens and comes to a complete boil.

4   Remove thickened custard from heat and add butter and extracts, stirring until the butter is melted completely and integrated. Transfer custard to a bowl and add four of the six sliced bananas to custard. Refrigerate covered custard until ready to construct your pudding.

5   Prepare pudding dessert: For the traditional variation I used to make at my old high school restaurant, layer a casserole dish with interchanging layers of custard and "Nilla" wafers feeling free to line the sides with cookies as well. I always make the first layer custard and go from there, but the choice is yours. Top final layer with vanilla wafers and 2 sliced bananas and serve with whipped cream. Makes 12 servings.

As I mention in my recipe for Glazed Tarte aux Baies, it is of the utmost importance that you remove the milk mixture from the heat of the stovetop when adding your egg mixture. The eggs function as the thickening agent, but they're still eggs. If you do this step too slowly and over a heat that's high, the eggs will cook the second they hit your boiling milk and you'll be left with a chunky custard that still tastes great, but will have large fat molecules throughout. If these chunks do occur, strain the custard through a kitchen mesh strainer to fix the problem.

Any-Season Crumble with Apricots
and Almonds

PERHAPS ONE OF the most versatile bakery items in this book remains this any-season crumble. Adapted here to my favorite summer produce, this breakfast (or dessert) item can be easily revised for any season of the year with the substitution of seasonal fruits: fall pears and apples, winter oranges, and/or spring strawberries and berries.

FILLING

4 cups apricots or any seasonal fruit, sliced

1 tablespoon flour

¾ cup sugar

CRUMBLE TOPPING

1 cup steel-cut oats, not instant

½ cup almonds, sliced

⅓ cup brown sugar, packed

1 teaspoon cinnamon

1 teaspoon allspice

¼ cup flour

½ stick butter, melted

1   Preheat oven to 350F. Prepare filling: Slice apricots and combine with flour and sugar. Pour fruit mixture into an ungreased casserole dish or pie pan.

2   Prepare crumble topping: Mix dry ingredients—oats, almonds, brown sugar, cinnamon, allspice, and flour with melted butter until mixture resembles a coarse meal. Sprinkle crumble mixture over fruit filling and bake for 35 minutes, or until crumble is golden brown and fruit mixture is warm and bubbly. Remove from oven and cool slightly. Serve warm with crème fraîche, whipped cream, yogurt, or ice cream. Makes 6 servings.

Watermelon Juice with Basil

"A WATERMELON IS my favorite thing to juice. Why? Well, because it's *all juice*," Tara, a smiling friend and what I would refer to as a "juice enthusiast," explained one hot June day.

A watermelon seemed like the strangest fruit to juice when I was first introduced to the idea—what on earth would watermelon juice taste like? Would it be as sweet as the fruity triangles I eat at picnics? Or, would it be watered-down like a bad smoothie? I just wasn't sure. Clearly, I hadn't yet tried the stuff.

Watermelon juice is . . . in one word, perfection. Pure perfection. Pure sunshine in a glass.

I'm so convinced of watermelon juice's perfection as a refreshing summer drink that I've fallen in love with the sweet and fruity red stuff and can't make enough of it. I keep whole pitchers of watermelon juice in my fridge, drinking up cold glasses after a long run at the LSU lakes or as a quick breakfast before I run out the door in the morning.

Move over lemonade; watermelon juice—fresh from the Louisiana sun and squeezed into a glass—is here to stay (at least in my kitchen). Try watermelon juice for the first time with this easy basil infusion or other alternatives like mint or lavender. Summer has never tasted so good!

Watermelon juice is a relatively easy drink to make if you own a juicer. However, watermelon can be juiced through a more basic method at home with the use of a plate, strainer, and oversized bowl. Read below for both techniques.

1 watermelon (large), removed from rind and cut into 1-inch cubes

½–1 cup basil, washed with small leaves reserved for garnish

½ teaspoon salt

½ teaspoon rice wine vinegar

WITH A JUICER:

1 Remove fruit from the rind and juice watermelon into a large pitcher with the help of a standard juicer. Juice pulp entirely until it's all juice. Add basil leaves to juicer and process into the same pitcher. Add salt and rice wine vinegar, mix to combine. Chill and serve with basil leaves to garnish.

NO-JUICER ALTERNATIVE:

1   Take an oversized bowl and place a strainer inside the bowl. Put watermelon in strainer and using a plate (or clean hands), press down on the watermelon until all of the watermelon's juice has drained into the bowl and just the red pulp remains in the strainer. Discard pulp and continue.

2   Add the basil: This step is a little trickier as you'll have to process the basil without the help of a juicer. I suggest using a food processor or blender just to get the basil into a paste and then mixing the paste directly into the juice. However, you'll want to go light on the basil here since you're using whole basil leaves as well as their juice. Process and add to bowl with the watermelon juice, salt, and vinegar. Mix to combine and serve chilled with basil leaves to garnish. Makes 12 servings.

Louisiana Bloody Marys

IN COLLEGE, I was never much of a drinker, but since moving to Baton Rouge for graduate school (and let's be honest, the food), I've found this preference to be a little hard to keep with all of the tailgating in the fall, the carnival in the spring, and the long hot nights in the summer.

With this new beverage culture, I've grown into a bit of a Bloody Mary drinker as well. But in Louisiana, the Bloody Marys are spicier, infused with Cajun spices along with other strange ingredients so that the mixture is blended to a pulpless sea of crimson perfection. It's one of the only times I drink red drinks, and it's the only time that I ever feel "fabulous" *after* drinking.

Recently suffering from the aftereffects of summer reveling, I looked in my fridge to the strangest of ingredients: olives, okra, celery, and tomato juice. I had planned on making Bloody Marys with my friends for Sunday brunch and boy, did I need it.

This hair of the dog and cultural hangover cure may very possibly be the only time tomato juice really ever tastes good . . . ever. And I tend to believe this drink tastes "extra good" here in Louisiana. Combine your traditional Bloody Mary with an array of spices, freshly squeezed juices, some Worcestershire sauce, and salt and pepper to taste. Rim the glasses with Tony Chachere's Cajun Seasoning—a popular salt and spice blend available anywhere—and start the recovery process.

3 cups tomato juice (fresh, from juiced tomatoes if you have them)

¼ cup fresh lemon juice (about 2 lemons, juiced)

¼ cup plus 3 tablespoons fresh lime juice

¼ cup cilantro, minced or finely chopped

1 to 2 jalapeños, to taste with stems removed and minced (with or without seeds)

1 tablespoon horseradish, finely chopped, or pre-prepared horseradish paste

2 cloves garlic, minced or pressed

1 tablespoon Worcestershire, or to taste

½ teaspoon salt

¼ teaspoon freshly ground black pepper

1½ cups vodka

To garnish: lime slices, celery stalks, okra, green olives, and Tony Chachere's Cajun Seasoning for the rim

1   Combine ingredients in a blender—tomato juice, lemon and lime juice, cilantro, jalapeños, horseradish, garlic, Worcestershire, salt, pepper, and vodka. Season to taste with more of the above. Refrigerate mixture for several hours before serving.

2   Serve in Tony Chachere's–rimmed glasses.

3   Add olives, okra, and celery, or lime slices to taste and enjoy! Makes 6 large (16-ounce) servings.

Louisiana Lemonade, including Pomegranate or
Strawberry Variation, and Limeade

GOOD HOMEMADE LEMONADE is a staple in my summer kitchen. On hot days when I feel like I'm always having to cut the grass, nothing says a job well done like this refreshing beverage.

The key to a great homemade lemonade recipe is to find the right balance of sweet and tangy flavors for your palette. I prefer my lemonade to have a little bite (as indicated by the lower amounts of sugar in the first version below), but an extra quarter- to half-cup of sugar can sweeten this variation easily.

Like any produce-inspired cook, I've adapted my regular go-to-lemonade to include several of my favorite fruits during the summertime—strawberries, pomegranates, and limes. Serve in tall glasses with plenty of ice to refresh your warm summer body or sip in smaller servings as an aperitif—a drink to stimulate the palette—before any light summer meal.

LEMONADE

1 cup lemon juice, freshly squeezed (about 4–6 lemons)

¾ cup sugar

1 cup water

4 cups water

LIMEADE

5–6 limes, juiced (1 cup lime juice, a little more or less)

¾ cup sugar

1 cup water

LEMONADE OR LIMEADE VARIATION

1 Prepare fruit juice: Squeeze enough lemons (or limes) for 1 cup of juice (about 4–6 lemons or 5–6 limes), using an old-fashioned hand-held juicer or standing electronic juicer, and reserve. For information on the best device for the job, see my "Kitchen Tools and Equipment List" as I advocate for the use of a handheld lemon squeezer for juicing here.

2 Prepare the simple syrup: In a nonstick saucepan set to medium heat, dissolve a 1:1 ratio of sugar and water (1 cup water and 1 cup sugar, but I prefer ¾ cup sugar based on personal preference) until sugar dissolves completely. Add fruit juice to sugar, stir, and remove from heat. Cool mixture slightly before transferring to a pitcher (especially a glass one).

3 Fill pitcher with remaining water, fruit-infused simple syrup, and taste after stirring. Adjust with more water or sugar as necessary. Refrigerate lemonade/limeade for at least half an hour before serving. Makes 4 servings.

POMEGRANATE LEMONADE

2 pomegranates, seeded

2 lemons, juiced

¾ cup sugar

1 cup water

STRAWBERRY LEMONADE

1 quart strawberries, pureed

2 lemons, juiced

1 cup sugar

1 cup water

POMEGRANATE LEMONADE

1   Probably one of the more difficult lemonades of the batch, this pomegranate drink has a distinct berry taste and a delightful red color. Follow the steps above for the simple syrup, but this time use only 2 lemons for the citrus-infused simple syrup. For juicing the berries, see my "Kitchen Tools/Equipment List" at the beginning of this book for how to use a mortar and pestle for the task of juicing pomegranate seeds. For more instructions, read over "Cooking Methods, Techniques, and Food Preservation" information on working with pomegranate seeds. When ready to juice berries, add berries to a standard kitchen mortar and pestle. Crush berries into a juice and pour into lemon-infused simple syrup before adding to water, mixing, and tasting. Refrigerate for at least 30 minutes before serving. Makes 4 servings.

STRAWBERRY LEMONADE

1   Follow steps 1–3 above making sure to use only 2 lemons for the simple syrup. When juicing the fruit, opt for blending the strawberry simple syrup mixture before adding it to a serving pitcher. Here's how:

2   Prepare simple syrup according to instructions, wash, de-stem, and halve strawberries. Add halved strawberries to simple syrup, remove from heat, and cool slightly. Process strawberry simple syrup in a blender or food processor until smooth. Combine simple syrup in a pitcher with remaining water. Mix and refrigerate for at least 30 minutes before serving. Makes 4 servings.

Watermelon Feta Salad Cakes

THE IDEA OF adding sweet juicy watermelon to a soft white cheese always surprises my dinner guests upon first sight. Like my favorite Watermelon Juice with Basil, this easy snack introduces another way to serve basil and watermelon together but without the pulsing of a beverage. The feta may seem like a surprising combination for these two, but watermelon and feta are actually a commonly paired duo in bright summer salads.

Together, white-bricked cheese and ruby red watermelon make a beautiful summer snack and the flavor is as bright as the colorful ingredients. Dress with shredded basil leaves and drizzled balsamic for a powerful palette starter or summer snack.

1 small watermelon, cut into circular rounds using an overturned glass

1 large feta block, cut into circular rounds using an overturned glass

1 bunch basil leaves, stemmed and washed

balsamic vinegar (blueberry, preferably), to dress

1   Remove watermelon from rind and cut into long, thick slices. Using an overturned glass, cookie cutter, or small cake ring, punch out circular rounds of watermelon and then plate.

2   Using the same technique above, punch out the same size (or smaller) feta rounds to serve with the watermelon. Top watermelon rounds with feta rounds, and dress with leaves of basil and drops of balsamic vinegar (blueberry if you have it) and serve. Makes 10–12 servings.

autumn

SEPTEMBER–NOVEMBER

The farther summer progresses, the more I look
forward to autumn produce with dreams of cool-
weather squashes, sweet potatoes, apples, and pears.
In terms of local availability of produce, autumn plays
a close second to my summer favorites by entering
with a bang. For the recipes that follow, I make use of
ripe pears in just about every kind of dish—appetizers,
salads, and desserts—and either find an easy way to
bake apples or convert them into post-dinner cocktails.
Sweet potatoes are reinvented in several new ways,
whereas easy chicken dishes inspire most of my entrées
as long as they are encrusted with Parmesan and
pumpkin seeds or stuffed with pancetta and croissants.
A little earthier and always fresh, fall produce brings
natural decadence to the table with seasonal squashes,
fruits, and herbs.

Sundried Tomato Hummus

Asian Pears with Honey, Gorgonzola, and
   Bourbon Candied Pecans

BBQ Meatball Sliders

Cheese-Stuffed Dates with Prosciutto

Easy Roasted Garlic with Thyme

Pear and Pancetta Salad

Rosemary's Rosemary Pumpkin Soup

Tomato Basil Soup

Herbed Chicken with Pancetta Croissant Stuffing

Pumpkin-Encrusted Chicken Parmesan

Pumpkin Sage Ravioli

Michael's Mac and Blue Cheese

Spiced Sweet Potatoes

Spaghetti Squash Roasted in Walnut Olive Oil,
   Garlic, and Parsley

Sweet Potatoes with Goat Cheese and
   Bourbon Candied Pecan Relish

Cranberry Sauce

Candied Pears (Dipped in Dark Chocolate
   and Chopped Pecans)

Poached Pears with Mint

Chocolate Cake with Red Wine Pears

Pumpkin Spice Bread Pudding

Stuffed Baked Apples with Rum

Boudin, Sundried Tomato, and Spinach Omelet

Cheesy Southern Biscuits

Hot Spiced Cider with Rum

Apple Ginger Ale Cocktail

Cajun-Spiced Pumpkin Seeds

APPETIZERS

Sundried Tomato Hummus

WHEN I THINK "hummus," I think, "breakfast, lunch, and dinner." That's how much I like this dip—it's more than a snack, it's a meal. In fact, it's the kind of meal I can eat for at least two days on end (and have *plenty* of times).

So here's a new take on an old favorite—my classic Hummus recipe, but with one noticeably different ingredient, sundried tomatoes. My recipe calls for sundried tomatoes that aren't jarred in olive oil, but naturally dried and oil-less. However, the ones in oil do work for making a creamier dish, though with less of the intended brightness of this dried fruit. If you must use sundried tomatoes that have been oil-packed, simply cut down on olive oil by one half. Oil-less tomatoes can be bought online or at specialty food stores along with tahini, a necessary sesame paste for this dish. For a link to these products and the original recipe, see the resources index in the back.

After the sweet ripe tomatoes of summer, sundried tomatoes offer summertime flavors in a different form. Process all of your ingredients together with the sundried tomatoes and voila! A hummus that is rich in flavor, color, and satisfaction. Before you know it, you'll be eating hummus for breakfast too.

2 (15-ounce) cans garbanzo beans, drained

¼ cup olive oil

4 cloves garlic, minced or pressed

⅔ cup tahini

½ cup water

⅓ cup freshly squeezed lemon juice

salt and pepper to taste

2–3 tablespoons parsley, chopped, to taste (plus extra for garnishing)

1 cup sundried tomatoes, chopped, with several reserved for garnishing

pine nuts, for garnishing

1 In a food processor, combine garbanzo beans, olive oil, pressed or minced garlic, tahini, water, lemon juice, and seasonings. Add sundried tomatoes. Process until smooth.

2 Taste to balance the hummus's palette—add more parsley and salt and pepper as necessary. Process a second time and taste.

3 Transfer to serving bowl and garnish with pine nuts, chopped sundried tomatoes, parsley, olive oil, and salt and pepper. Serve with any number of dipping items—pita, cucumbers, tomatoes, and bell peppers. Makes 12–14 servings.

Asian Pears with Honey, Gorgonzola, and Bourbon Candied Pecans

SOMETIMES THE BEST hors d'oeuvres and desserts are the most undemanding and the freshest. Many foodies get caught up in the cooking process of fancy gadgets, exotic ingredients, and tons of effort. Although I've been known to wield a cherry pitter on occasion, I've become an increasing fan of minimalism in the kitchen. Merely chop crisp fresh produce, dress it with basic pantry ingredients, and voila! An effortless, clearly delicious hors d'oeuvre or treat.

This recipe serves delicious Asian pear hors d'oeuvres with Gorgonzola, bourbon candied pecans, and honey. My first of two recipes inspired by my friend Michael Agan.

Michael has the best sense of what is *good* when it comes to fresh cooking. He knows how to combine flavors, cut prices, and create impressive presentations that dazzle any appetite. His idea for this recipe combines fall pears with your typical cheesy appetizer, but brings it to a whole other level with the combination of nuts and honey. Michael's original version used walnuts, but I've swapped them out for a candy-like alternative: my Bourbon Candied Pecans from the winter section of this book. This flavorful, healthy, Asian pear combination gets its tastiness from the honey and cheese, while the pear and pecans add a satisfying fall crunch to the dish.

Although Michael prefers red Asian pears to green ones and suggests the use of Gorgonzola, walnuts, and honey, this versatile hors d'oeuvre can be adjusted to candied or regular pecans, and another syrup (such as maple), and to blue cheese or even a vegan-friendly cheese. Don't have pears? Substitute fresh fall apples.

4–6 red Asian pears

¼ cup honey

¼ cup Gorgonzola cheese, crumbled

¼ cup Bourbon Candied Pecans, whole, or chopped (recipe found in the Winter Appetizers section)

1 Wash pears and remove stems. Using a paring knife, cut each pear into small, length-wise, bite-size pieces and then plate. Remove seeds.

2 Drizzle pears with honey, and add crumbled Gorgonzola and bourbon candied pecans and serve. Makes 4–6 servings.

BBQ Meatball Sliders

YET ANOTHER RECIPE developed from the sausage I received from Marx Foods (see Summer, Grilled Sausage): extra-savory fine sausage portioned in slider-size meatballs on toasted rolls with melted cheese for an extra satisfying appetizer in a bite-size form.

Barbeque sauce isn't a "fresh" ingredient per se, but Louisiana is home to some of the most flavorful sauces I've had. Made locally, Louisiana barbeque sauces infuse spicy peppers with sweet ingredients like amber honeys or raspberries for a traditional Cajun kick at any summer party. Many stores in Louisiana stock spicy pork as a popular favorite as well.

½ pound ground beef

½ pound ground spicy pork (substitute regular pork + 2 tablespoons cayenne, chili powder, or Louisiana hot sauce)

¼ cup bread crumbs

¼ cup Parmesan cheese,

1 egg + 1 egg yolk

1 teaspoon kosher salt

¼ cup parsley, chopped fine

½ cup BBQ sauce of your choice (I prefer local BBQ sauces like Jack Miller's, just as long as it's *spicy*)

1 teaspoon cayenne or chili powder

TO DRESS SLIDERS:

regular or whole grain rolls, halved and toasted

provolone cheese

arugula, or other leafy green

Can't find spicy pork? Add 2 tablespoons cayenne, homemade chili powder, or Louisiana hot sauce to the meatball mixture for a flavorful variation.

1   In a large bowl, combine beef, pork, bread crumbs, Parmesan, egg and egg yolk, salt, parsley, BBQ sauce, and cayenne to integrate fully. Form mixture into 3-inch meatballs (about 12).

2   In a large nonstick skillet, add half of the meatballs, making sure not to crowd the pan. Fry meatballs until brown all over and cooked all the way through. Avoid the urge to flatten meatballs as you want them to keep their "ball" shape.

3   Plate cooked meatballs and drain excess oil and brush with any leftover BBQ sauce. Serve on toasted rolls with provolone cheese, arugula, and spear with toothpicks and serve. Makes 12 sliders.

Cheese-Stuffed Dates with Prosciutto

DATES ARE ONE of those sweet summertime ingredients that—like figs—do well on everything from salads to antipasti to plain hors d'oeuvres. By themselves, the exotic flavor of the fruit pairs nicely with the salt content of a savory dried meat like pancetta or prosciutto. Stuff with goat cheese for a rich triangulation that wows.

24 Medjool dates (18 ounces), pitted

4 ounces goat cheese, semisoft

4 ounces prosciutto, cut into thin slices

salt and pepper, to taste

1   Using a paring knife, make a small incision down the long side of each date and stuff with semisoft goat cheese until full (about ½–1 teaspoon cheese, depending on the size of your dates).

2   Wrap dates in thin slices of prosciutto and spear with toothpicks. Plate and sprinkle dates *lightly* with salt and pepper and serve. Makes 24 dates.

Easy Roasted Garlic with Thyme

ALWAYS ABUNDANT, WHOLE garlic bulbs make for impressive appetizers when slow-roasted to savory perfection. Roasted inside their casing, garlic bulbs press out easily onto crackers, crusty bread, or slow-roasted vegetables. Creating an impressive presentation that requires very little work, these Easy Roasted Garlics with Thyme can be baked inside a muffin pan, on a well-greased baking sheet, or inside aluminum foil.

6 bulbs garlic

4 tablespoons olive oil (I prefer Walnut-Infused Olive Oil from Fioré)

1 teaspoon thyme, chopped fine

coarse salt, such as kosher or sea, and pepper, to taste

1 Preheat oven to 350F. Peel garlic down to its last few thin layers of paper-like skin making sure not to over peel as the bulbs may not stay intact after cooking.

2 Using a chef's knife, cut off the pointed top of each garlic bulb (about ½ inch from the tip).

3 Place garlic in muffin tins with cut side facing up and drizzle a little less than 1 tablespoon olive oil across the top of each bulb. Season with coarse salt, pepper, and thyme.

4 Roast garlic in oven for 35–40 minutes, or until bulbs are tender to the pressure of a fork or toothpick. Remove from oven and cool slightly. Plate and serve with bread items such as a baguette, crackers, or other crusty French bread. Makes 6 bulbs.

Roasted garlic is one of those easy kitchen ingredients that work fabulously as an appetizer as suggested here, but also go great flavoring side dishes, entrées, or any other item. Often, I mash holiday potatoes with a bulb of roasted garlic, or serve them on top of a rib eye steak.

Pear and Pancetta Salad

SOMETHING ABOUT THE combination of the words "pear" with "pancetta" just sounds absolutely lovely. Typically served with sweet honeys and dark chocolates, pears are the less-crisp cousins of fall apples with milder tones of sweetness. Yet their soft and juicy texture makes me absolutely love them, and I cannot think of a better way to bring an unimaginative bed of spinach to life than with this ripe fruit.

For this salad recipe, I have steered away from the traditionally sweet methods of preparing cold-weather pears for a saltier variation that highlights the natural sugars of the fruit itself. Served on a bed of spinach, pears cozy up nicely to salty Italian bacon meats like pancetta for an easy salad with instant sophistication. Don't have pancetta? Try a slice or two of crisped bacon for an introduction to this sweet and salty blend.

Use pre-cubed fried pancetta to add crispy texture and instant flavor to any winter salad. Served over a bed of ripe pears, spinach, and a sprinkling of balsamic vinegar, pancetta upgrades any salad with just the right amount of salt. "Pear" and "pancetta" have never sounded lovelier.

2 cups spinach, packed

1 Asian pear, cored and cut into slices

1 ounce pancetta, fried and crisped

2 tablespoons Parmesan

3 tablespoons Cinnamon Pear Balsamic Vinegar from Fioré

1 Wash 2 cups spinach and plate. Using a sharp paring knife, cut a ripe Asian pear in half, core, and cut fruit into slices making sure to remove seeds. Plate slices on top of spinach bed.

2 In a small nonstick skillet over medium heat, crisp up pancetta until crispy. Sprinkle pancetta over spinach and pears, making sure to use any excess fat rendered during the frying process to dress the spinach (this technique is referred to as "wilting" a salad).

3 Sprinkle salad with Parmesan and balsamic vinegar (my favorite being the Cinnamon Pear Balsamic Vinegar from Fioré) and serve. Makes 1 serving.

Rosemary's Rosemary Pumpkin Soup

HANDING ME A sticky note akin to a grocery list—"Pumpkin (small), green onions, bread crumbs, gruyère, and broth"—my friend Dr. Rosemary Peters offered me the most innovative pumpkin recipe ever to grace "Pumpkin Week" at Clearly Delicious: pumpkin soup served hot and bubbly inside a self-cooking pumpkin bowl and topped with melted cheese. Eating out of a pumpkin as a bowl? And, eating the pumpkin? My interest was stimulated by this easy, yet curiously constructed pumpkin soup.

This is not your average cold-weather soup, but innovation at its finest. Here, the pumpkin serves as both a bowl and main ingredient. Warm broth steams the pumpkin when baking while also retaining the gourd-like shape upon serving. Spoon in hand, your dinner companions can dig into the pumpkin as they enjoy the broth. The combination of steamed pumpkin and broth thickened by cheese, bread crumbs, and herbs introduces an avant-garde take on October soups.

My version follows Rosemary's ingredients list with a few additions: I've added Parmesan and rosemary, but Gruyère cheese goes fantastically here along with other substitutions such as thyme or basil to complement the soup. Serve with crusty French bread for a real treat as lunch on a cool afternoon, or as a first course for a larger dinner party. Not only is the pumpkin cute and adorable, but the flavors and hardy pumpkin texture are also perfect for this fall weather.

1 teaspoon parsley, chopped fine

1–2 tablespoons rosemary, to taste

2 green onions, finely chopped

1 small baking pumpkin (sugar pumpkin), capped and seeded

broth (chicken, vegetable, or beef), enough to fill up the pumpkin

⅓ cup bread crumbs

2 cloves garlic, minced or pressed

salt and pepper, to taste

1 Preheat oven to 350F. Chop parsley, rosemary, and green onions. Remove the pumpkin's cap and scoop out excess fibrous filling and seeds. You want the pumpkin to be "clean" before baking it.

2 Fill pumpkin to the top with broth, parsley, rosemary, green onions, bread crumbs, minced or pressed garlic, salt, pepper, and grated cheese on top.

3 Place pumpkin with top on in a circular baking sheet (I used a pie pan) and bake in oven for 45 minutes to an hour (or, until pumpkin appears to have softened and broth has reduced by a little more than ¼).

4 Remove pumpkin from oven and uncover. Allow pumpkin to sit for about 5 minutes before serving with crusty French bread. Makes 1 entrée serving or 2 appetizer servings.

Tomato Basil Soup

I MUST ADMIT, when it gets cold, seriously cold in Louisiana, I get a little cranky. One of the perks of living in one of the southernmost states is the warm weather all year round. Without fail, I've experienced 75F Decembers, hot and humid Thanksgivings, and coat-less birthdays (my birthday happens to be in January).

Despite the reliably good weather in Louisiana, cold snaps do happen. Driving my Vespa to campus, I feel like a human icicle, and no amount of hot coffee can keep me warm. This weather inspires the best of soups and I had to revisit my favorite Tomato Basil Soup recipe from back when Clearly Delicious was a blogging baby. A fabulous tomato soup recipe by Tyler Florence over at Food Network originally inspired my version of Tomato Basil Soup. For Tyler's Ultimate Tomato Basil Soup, see the link to Food Network available in the electronic resources at the back of this book.

But, for today's soup, my fresh Louisiana variation is just a little bit better—roasted vine ripe tomatoes (instead of canned) are pulsed together with fresh basil and chicken broth, and all I can do is smile. Eating my soup, I get to curl up in a ball with a good cookbook and for some reason, I don't feel so cranky anymore. . . .

4 pounds vine ripe tomatoes

2 yellow onions, small, sliced

½ cup chopped basil

6 cloves garlic, peeled

½ cup extra virgin olive oil (basil olive oil if you have it)

Italian seasoning, to taste (about 1–2 tablespoons)

salt and pepper, to taste (I prefer Tony Chachere's Cajun Seasoning and cracked pepper)

1 quart chicken stock (about 4 cups)

2–5 bay leaves

4 tablespoons butter

½ cup–¾ cup heavy cream

1   Preheat oven to 450F. Wash tomatoes, cut in half, and quarter.

2   Add quartered tomatoes to a roasting pan along with sliced onions, chopped basil, and half of the garlic. Drizzle with olive oil and season with Italian seasoning and salt and pepper, to taste.

3   Roast vegetables in oven until caramelized (about 20–30 minutes, depending on your stove).

4   Remove vegetables from stove and cool for several minutes. Transfer to a food processor and process for about 10–15 seconds.

5   Meanwhile, add chicken stock, bay leaves, and butter to a large pot and bring to a boil. Add pureed tomato mixture and stir to combine. Bring to a second boil. Reduce heat and add cream. Taste and adjust spices according to personal preference. Serve immediately with crusty bread or a grilled cheese sandwich. Makes 8 servings.

ENTRÉES

Herbed Chicken with Pancetta
Croissant Stuffing

A RELIABLE ROASTED chicken with seasonal herbs never fails to transition me from the smokier flavors of summer—as with my spring Beer Can Chicken, also great in summer—to the more earthy flavors of fall. Since herbed chicken goes wonderfully with just about any meal, I suggest impressing dinner guests with a side ingredient that threatens to steal the place of main dish: oven-roasted stuffing (what south Louisianans refer to as "dressing") made from buttery croissants and salty pancetta. Any buttery croissant and store-bought pancetta offers a lovely base for this recipe, but feel free to halve the croissants with the traditional addition of French bread.

A new conception of the turkey and dressing you'll be eating come November, this dish may just become a new seasonal tradition.

Special equipment needed: Dutch oven.

CHICKEN

1 (4–5) pound chicken

2 tablespoons rosemary, finely chopped

2 tablespoons thyme, finely chopped

2 tablespoons parsley, finely chopped

2 tablespoons basil, finely chopped

coarse salt and pepper, for rubbing

4 cups chicken broth, or enough to cover bird inside Dutch oven

1 bulb garlic, peeled

1   Preheat oven to 350F.

2   Prepare chicken: Using a paring knife, remove wishbone from bird. This step is a bit tricky, as you'll need to feel around for the bone. The best tip is to reach inside the bird from the neck cavity and carve the meat around the wishbone with a small knife until the bone comes loose and can be easily removed. Removing the wishbone before cooking makes carving the bird significantly easier. *You'll be glad you didn't skip this step.*

3   Chop herbs and toss with salt and pepper in a large bowl. Rub bird all over with herbs, salt, and pepper. Make sure not to rub just the outside of the bird, but the inside cavities as well.

STUFFING

1 teaspoon thyme, finely chopped

1 teaspoon rosemary, finely chopped

1 teaspoon basil, finely chopped

1 teaspoon parsley

½ onion, chopped fine

2 green onions, chopped

6 ounces pancetta, chunked into pieces

8 croissants, torn into pieces

4 tablespoons olive oil (basil olive oil if you have it)

8 tablespoons chicken broth

salt and pepper, to taste

4   In a large Dutch oven, place chicken with enough broth to barely cover the bird (about 4 cups, depending on the depth and width of your pot). Add garlic to the broth, cover pot, and cook bird for 1 hour on medium-high, or until juices have just barely evaporated. Remove bird from heat and keep warm in pot until ready to serve with stuffing.

5   Prepare stuffing: Chop herbs—thyme, rosemary, basil, and parsley—and set aside for stuffing. Finely chop onion and green onion. Chunk pancetta into irregular-size pieces.

6   Tear croissants into bite-size pieces and add to a greased casserole dish. In a nonstick skillet over medium heat, add onions to olive oil and sauté until tender. Right when onions begin to brown, add chunked pieces of pancetta and sauté until crispy. Remove onion pancetta mixture from heat and spread over croissants.

7   Sprinkle croissant mixture with herbs and salt and pepper. Mix to combine and roast until golden brown and cooked, about 20–25 minutes. Serve dressing with carved herb chicken. Makes 4–6 servings.

Pumpkin-Encrusted Chicken Parmesan

ONE FALL, A FRIEND served me pumpkin seed–encrusted tilapia for dinner. Never having used pumpkin seeds for anything besides a seasonal snack, I instantly fell in love with the versatility of the ingredient for encrusting fish, various kinds of poultry, and chicken breasts. For dishes with great sauces, pumpkin fits in nicely with the savory nature of the meal by adding a subtle earthy flavor reminiscent of fall.

This recipe adds a favorite fall flavor, pumpkin, to an easy home-cooked meal. Unsure of the addition of pumpkin seeds? Prepare chicken with only half of the seeds suggested for a sample taste test.

TOMATO SAUCE

1 onion, chopped fine

1 tablespoon basil, chopped fine

1 teaspoon thyme, chopped fine

3 cloves garlic, minced or pressed

2–3 tablespoons olive oil

1 (28-ounce) can roasted tomatoes

salt and pepper, to taste

1   Prepare tomato sauce: Chop onion, basil, thyme, and mince or press garlic. In a saucepan, warm olive oil and add onions. Cook onions until translucent and golden (about 5–8 minutes). Add garlic and stir until fragrant (about thirty seconds). Pour in tomatoes, thyme, basil, and season with salt and pepper to taste. Bring sauce to a simmer and cook over medium heat for about 10 minutes covered so that flavors absorb and the sauce reduces.

2   Prepare chicken: Preheat oven to 350F, and sprinkle four chicken breasts with kosher or sea salt generously on both sides. Let chicken tenderize for 10 minutes while sauce is cooking. For more information on how this process works, see recipe for Sirloin (or other) Steak with Herb Butter and (possibly) Egg in the Summer section of this book.

3   In a large bowl, whisk together eggs. In a separate bowl, combine bread crumbs, pumpkin seeds, salt, pepper, and half of the Parmesan. Warm olive oil in nonstick saucepan and turn off heat for tomato sauce. Rinse chicken breasts to remove any tenderizing salt and pat dry.

CHICKEN PARMESAN

4 chicken breasts (about 4 ounces each)

kosher salt, for tenderizing

2 eggs

¼ cup bread crumbs

¼ cup pumpkin seeds, toasted

salt and pepper, to taste

1 cup Parmesan, freshly grated

¼ cup olive oil

½ cup basil leaves, whole

cup mozzarella cheese

¼ cup basil, chopped fine

4 Dredge chicken through egg mixture and then toss in dry mixture to encrust and coat. Place coated chicken breasts in nonstick saucepan and cook on both sides for 4–5 minutes, or until golden brown.

5 Pour tomato sauce in a large casserole dish and sprinkle with half of the basil.

6 Place stovetop chicken breasts in casserole dish, making sure to spoon 1–2 tablespoons of the tomato sauce on top of each breast. Sprinkle with remaining Parmesan, basil, and mozzarella. Bake Chicken Parmesan in oven for 25–30 minutes or until cheese is golden on top. Serve with crusty Ciabatta Bread from the Winter Lagniappe section of this book. Makes 4 servings.

Pumpkin Sage Ravioli

THE SAGE IN my garden is the one herb that I can trust will be there all year round. Like rosemary, sage has a certain vivacity, which means, in part, that it grows like a weed, and also that I can't possibly kill it. In Louisiana, the weather seldom drops below 30 degrees in the winter, so I know my sage will always be safe. Staring across my garden bed vis-à-vis to my rosemary plant, sage and rosemary look like soldiers ready to wait out the Louisiana cold knowing that not too long from now it will be warm again.

I have yet to determine whether it's loyalty or stubbornness that allows this herb to grow so well in my back yard with little sun. Sage has a beautiful perfume and since no fall vegetable is more hardheaded than a squash or pumpkin, I have embraced these complementary spirits and flavors in this dish. Sage's aromatic leaves flavor the gourd-like pumpkin harvests of Louisiana's fall, and together, the two make for the best of friends.

Pumpkin makes for an unlikely filling when preparing ravioli, but one bite of my new fall favorite and you'll never go back. The recipe below calls for a simple pumpkin filling, but you can add even more seasonal variety to the dish by halving the filling with a serving of mashed acorn squash or sweet potato.

My Pumpkin Sage Ravioli is the ultimate comfort food. Just as the weather is getting cooler and pumpkin-everything is popping up everywhere, I suggest a bold take on traditional cheese or meat ravioli. Vegetarian in nature, this dish offers a hardy filling that's deeply flavorful. Between the decadent butter and cream sauce infused with more sage, basil, and Parmesan, you just might forget how stubborn your dinner companions are.

Looking to save time? Skip the homemade pasta for pre-cooked lasagna sheets as suggested with "Cooking Methods, Techniques and Food Preservation" at the beginning of this book. Special equipment needed: ravioli press or any overturned glass.

See kitchen gadgets in my "Cooking Methods, Techniques, and Food Preservation" section for more information about the wonders of homemade pasta.

PASTA

3½ cups all-purpose flour

1 teaspoon olive oil

1 teaspoon salt

5 large eggs

FILLING

1 cup organic pumpkin puree

1 cup Parmesan, shredded

1 teaspoon nutmeg

2 teaspoons sage, chopped fine

salt and pepper, to taste

SAUCE

1 stick salted butter

¾ cup cream

¾ cup Parmesan

salt and pepper, to taste

1 teaspoon basil, finely chopped

1 teaspoon sage, finely chopped

toasted pumpkin seeds, to garnish

1. In a standing mixer, attach the dough hook and combine flour, olive oil, salt, and eggs for three minutes until a dough ball forms. Cover with plastic wrap and rest for thirty minutes at room temperature.

2. Meanwhile, prepare the filling: Combine pumpkin, Parmesan, nutmeg, sage, and salt and pepper in a bowl. Mix to combine and taste. Add more salt and pepper as necessary.

3. Using a rolling pin and a well-floured surface, roll out dough as thinly as you possibly can. It's essential that when making ravioli, you do a single pass through with the pasta processing; otherwise, the dough will be tough and so will the ravioli. So, roll out the dough as thinly as possible and place teaspoon-size dollops of filling evenly throughout. I use my ravioli press as a stencil by making indentations into the dough and then, filling them with pumpkin. This way, I have a marker for how many pieces I will be making and never run out of dough.

4. Carefully fold half of the dough on top of itself and press down the edges, making a note of where each filling dollop is placed. Using a single ravioli press, punch out the individual squares (or circles) for each piece. Transfer to a plate lined with parchment paper and repeat until all of the dough has been used.

5. Bring a pot of salty water to a boil and add ravioli. Boil until *al dente*—firmly done, but still tender—which will take longer given the thickness of this particular pasta. For me, this step can take as long as 15 minutes.

6. While ravioli is cooking, prepare butter and cream sauce. Melt butter into a small saucepan and whisk cream, Parmesan, salt, pepper, basil, and sage to combine.

7. Strain ravioli and serve dressed in sauce, fresh Parmesan, toasted pumpkin seeds, basil, and sage. Makes 4 servings.

Michael's Mac and Blue Cheese

MY SECOND ODE to my friend Michael Agan's cooking skills comes in the form of this rich and sinful macaroni and cheese recipe. I've made the dish endless times with success, but it's never as delicious as when Michael prepares it for me. Adapted from a favorite macaroni and cheese recipe his mother made for many years, Michael's version adds blue cheese to the sauce for a stimulating flavor not fit for finicky five-year-olds.

When he told his mother about the change to her classic dish, she responded, "You added *bleu cheese* to *my* macaroni?!" All Michael could do was laugh, and I think of this story every time I make his version of macaroni and cheese. Michael's recipe calls for 1½ cups blue cheese, but cheddar can easily be swapped for 1 or ½ cup blue or Gorgonzola cheese for a less robust variation with more traditional cheddar flavor. Macaroni and Blue Cheese definitely isn't your mother's macaroni and cheese, and it may just be a *little* bit better.

4 strips bacon, chunked

1 pound penne pasta

2 tablespoons butter

¼ cup flour

2 cups whole milk

1 cup whipping cream

3 cups cheddar cheese, grated

1½ cups blue or Gorgonzola cheese, crumbled

1 Preheat oven to 350F. Butter a 13 × 9 casserole dish. Chunk bacon and cook until *crispy.*

2 Cook pasta in a large pot of salted boiling water until tender but still *al dente.* Drain and leave in strainer until the sauce is ready. Do not rinse with cold water.

3 Melt butter in a large saucepan over medium heat. Add flour to make a roux, whisking constantly to let the flour cook but not burn.

4 Gradually whisk in milk and cream. Simmer until mixture thickens, whisking constantly. Reduce heat to low and add grated cheddar cheese (reserving ½ cup for sprinkling on top before baking) and crumbled blue cheese. Whisk until cheese melts (about 2 minutes) and season to taste with salt and pepper.

5   Add cooked pasta to sauce, stir, and coat. Transfer mixture to pre-
    pared baking pan and sprinkle with remaining cheddar cheese. Bake
    until golden brown on top [sauce will begin to bubble], about 25
    minutes. Remove from oven and allow to rest for at least 5 minutes.
    Serve warm. Makes 8 servings.

Cold water counteracts the temperature-necessary cooking effects
of working with hot, freshly made pasta. Although some dishes require cold-water baths when working with macaroni, this is not one
of them.

SIDE DISHES

Spiced Sweet Potatoes

WHEN MID-OCTOBER ROLLS around every fall, I start experimenting. The next two months are some of the busiest culinary experiences I have all year, and I want to develop recipes that wow my dinner guests.

I'm always looking for new takes on holiday favorites. Some way to infuse pumpkin into every dish I make, or peppermint into the most unlikely of desserts. But really, what desserts don't get a little something from peppermint?

But first, let's start simple. Take those holiday classics that we all know and love and make them a bit . . . different. Infuse a certain "je ne sais quoi" into our ingredients lists so that when someone takes their first bite of that new dish you've made, they'll have to ask, "Wow. This tastes great. What's in it?"

Most sweet potato recipes call for a ton of holiday spices—ginger, cinnamon, nutmeg, allspice, and more. But rarely do we ever see sweet potatoes with nuttier flavors (sans my Aunt Cathy's Sweet Potato Soufflé with Candied Pecans). I've infused this recipe with an almond-flavored butter that packs a seriously sophisticated punch, but goes so naturally with our favorite traditional spices this time of year.

For my Spiced Sweet Potatoes, our little secret is almonds. Butter infused with almond extract to be exact. I can't believe I haven't tried this combination before. The sweet earthy candied potatoes mixed with a nutty almond flavor wows every time I make it. AND, it doesn't stray too far from the traditional recipes we all know and love.

Since it's fall, enjoy the experimenting!

4 pounds sweet potatoes

½ cup brown sugar, packed

1 teaspoon nutmeg

1 teaspoon cinnamon

1 teaspoon allspice

1 stick butter, room temperature

2 tablespoons almond extract

salt and pepper, to taste

1   Wash sweet potatoes and wrap in aluminum foil. Pierce with a fork and bake until tender all the way through (375F for one hour and 15 minutes). Remove potatoes from oven and cool.

2   When cool to the touch, but still warm, peel potatoes and dump into a standing mixer with the paddle attachment.

3   Add sugar, nutmeg, cinnamon, and allspice. In a small saucepan melt one stick butter with 2 tablespoons almond extract and simmer for five minutes over low heat. Pour infused butter over sweet potato mixture and combine all ingredients on medium speed. Taste and adjust with any salt or pepper and serve warm. Makes 8 servings.

Spaghetti Squash Roasted in Walnut Olive Oil, Garlic, and Parsley

"THIS TASTES LIKE chicken! Oh my god . . . oh my god . . . is there chicken in this?!" my dinner companion—who just so happens to be a vegetarian—incoherently muttered half in joy and, well, half in confusion.

Sometimes miracles happen in the kitchen. Sometimes ingredients come together so perfectly that they create their own fireworks show of tastes, smells, and flavors. Sometimes squash, well, sometimes squash can taste like chicken.

And might I add this chicken incident was a complete accident. Having recently found a beautiful spaghetti squash at Southside Produce Market (off Perkins in Baton Rouge), I knew I finally had the perfect vegetable item to sauté in my Walnut-Infused Olive Oil from Fioré.

Most people prepare spaghetti squash with an easy, simple (and satisfying) garlic and butter sauté, but I refuse to believe these are our only options for this handsome cold-weather squash. Instead, I believe squash should be served nutty (just like butternut squash with pecans) and not masked by butter, or garlic, but enhanced by it.

Thus—a warm, nutty, spaghetti squash sauté was born out of a few simple ingredients. Combine roasted spaghetti squash with fresh, chopped parsley, minced or pressed garlic, some mozzarella, and my favorite earthy winter olive oil infused with walnuts from France. Season to taste. The result? A squash that tastes warm and delicious (just as it should be) with a hint of mozzarella and walnuts, or . . . a hint of "chicken."

Don't have walnut olive oil? Simmer olive oil with ½ cup walnuts before adding to squash (strain walnuts from oil before using, or simply add the walnuts with your oil to the dish).

1 large spaghetti squash

¼ cup chopped parsley (reserve some to garnish)

salt and pepper to taste

4 cloves garlic, minced or pressed

¼ cup mozzarella, shredded

2 tablespoons butter

2–3 tablespoons walnut-infused olive oil

1   Preheat oven to 350F. Place squash on roasting pan (whole) and cook for one hour.

2   Remove squash from oven and check for doneness: Using a sharp knife, press against the skin to see if it pierces. If the skin gives way without much pressure from the knife, then your squash is done.

3   Cut squash in half and remove seeds with a spoon. Using the same spoon, scoop out the insides of the squash and transfer to a bowl. At this point, the squash will become stringy instantly and begin to resemble spaghetti.

4   Add almost all of the parsley (reserving some to garnish), salt and pepper (to taste), garlic, and mozzarella. Mix and toss to combine.

5   In a deep, oversized saucepan or Dutch oven, add butter and walnut-infused olive oil. Melt down butter and add squash mixture to pan. Mix to coat squash fully in butter and olive oil and sauté for about five minutes. Taste for flavor and doneness, then serve warm with parsley and cracked pepper to garnish. Makes 6–8 servings.

Sweet Potatoes with Goat Cheese and
Bourbon Candied Pecan Relish

IMAGINE A MEAL that's naturally sweet, but not by sugar. A meal that has a satisfying crunch and the aftertaste of sharp, flavorful goat cheese. A meal that balances salty and sweet in the most surprising ways that you have no idea what you are eating, but boy, is it pretty.

These were the first impressions I experienced when I prepared this out-of-the-box take on baked sweet potatoes. I love baked sweet potatoes with the skin on, but combined with a fresh vegetable relish made from sweet dried cranberries, bourbon candied pecans, and goat cheese? Now this dish was one I *had* to try. Don't get me wrong, I love sweet potatoes about as much as Oprah, but not in the way you might expect. I prefer sweet potatoes to have a subtle tang alongside our traditionally sweet alternatives for preparing the vegetable. Although chefs rarely add anything but butter and sugar to sweet potatoes, savory cheeses like goat cheese complement sweet potatoes well.

Not a fan of goat cheese? Skip the ingredient and prepare the relish by itself for an equally satisfying variation of traditional baked sweet potato coins.

---

2 pounds sweet potato, scrubbed, unpeeled, cut into ¾-to-1-inch "coins"

salt and pepper

2 stalks celery, chopped fine

1 green onion, minced

¼ cup toasted Bourbon Candied Pecan Halves (recipe in the Winter Appetizers section)

3 tablespoons flat leaf parsley, chopped fine

1   Preheat oven to 450F. Wash potatoes thoroughly. Cut potatoes into ¾-to-1-inch "coins." Place potatoes on an oiled baking sheet.

2   Sprinkle with salt and pepper. Roast for 15 minutes on one side and flip for an additional 10 minutes on the other side. Remove from oven when done.

3   Prepare the "salsa": Chop celery, green onion, toasted pecan halves, and parsley. Add to a bowl with one teaspoon dried cranberries. Mix to combine.

1½ tablespoons dried cranberries ("craisins")

3 tablespoons olive oil

2 teaspoons red wine vinegar

½ teaspoon Dijon mustard

½ teaspoon Worcestershire sauce

2 ounces goat cheese

4   In a separate bowl, add olive oil, vinegar, Dijon, and Worcestershire sauce. Whisk to combine and add to chopped ingredients. Mix to combine.

5   Plate sweet potatoes and dress with salsa and goat cheese (if using). One teaspoon salsa for most smaller-size potatoes will do, but more if the potato coins are larger. If using soft goat cheese, cut cheese into small pieces and garnish the top of each potato before serving. Makes 4 servings.

Cranberry Sauce

I WILL ALWAYS be a sucker for cranberry sauce IN a can. You know—the kind where it "plops" onto a plate and can be cut based on the ringlet indentations made from the tin? Just thinking about this nuclear family favorite makes me think of everything Thanksgiving.

But the cranberry sauce in a can isn't *real* cranberry sauce. It's mostly sugar, food coloring, and water combination akin to Jell-O with very little cranberries. (Honestly, what do you expect for 27 cents a can?)

But the real thing, *real* cranberry sauce is almost dessert-like in nature. It has a delicious consistency of ripe berries and gooey sauce while being simultaneously sweet and sour. My recipe for homemade cranberry sauce incorporates the zest of one lemon and a tablespoon of cinnamon. The lemon adds a surprisingly bright citrus taste and the cinnamon encompasses all things holiday. I just love it.

No matter how old I get, I will always serve cranberry sauce in a can. But next to it—in a much fancier serving dish—will be this recipe for the homemade variation. The sauce tastes like any traditional cranberry holiday concoction, but incorporates a touch of lemon and cinnamon to give it that certain gourmet quality. Serve both at your next Thanksgiving or Christmas dinner and take a vote for your dinner companions' favorites. Maybe they'll have trouble choosing too. . . .

Want to sweeten things up? Consider substituting an orange's zest with a little juice for the lemon suggested below.

1 (12-ounce) bag of fresh
cranberries, washed

zest of 1 lemon

1 cup sugar

1 cup water

1 tablespoon cinnamon

1   Wash cranberries and set aside. Zest 1 lemon and reserve.

2   In a large pan, combine sugar and water. Bring to a boil, whisking occasionally so that the sugar dissolves. Once it boils, add lemon zest, cinnamon, and cranberries.

3   Bring mixture to another boil and cover pot with lid. Reduce heat and allow to simmer for 10–15 minutes, or until each of the berries has popped. Trust me, you'll want to cover your pot at this step; otherwise you may have a red cranberry juice/white stove situation.

4   Turn off heat and cool. Transfer sauce to a serving dish and either serve immediately or refrigerate. Sauce lasts for up to 1 month refrigerated. Makes 8–10 servings.

DESSERTS

Candied Pears (Dipped in Dark Chocolate and Chopped Pecans)

EVERY GROWN WOMAN has that one treat she just can't say "no" to. For me, it's candy apples. I just love them. Their crunchy sugary outside and the crisp sweet apples underneath are quintessential fall flavors for me (and my childhood). Chocolate and nuts have always been a favorite candied apple topping, and I am always a goner if I see this combination at a seasonal fair. Not only will I eat that candy apple, but I will also make a mess, looking happily on as my friends watch me ravish my favorite treat. I can attest that candied apples aren't just for kids!

While recently strolling the aisles of my local produce market, I picked up red pears by mistake. I was talking with a friend and assumed what I was bagging what were very large (albeit awkwardly shaped) red apples. You can imagine my surprise when, upon melting chocolate and chopping nuts for my favorite fall recipe, I discovered Asian pears were waiting in my grocery bag.

Since these things do happen, and I love all kinds of candied fruit, I suggest trying a fabulously fresh idea on the traditional candy apple—Candied Pears. Ripe red pears are softer than their crispy apple counterparts and the combination of dark chocolate and chopped pecans taste like fall. The flavor will astound you, the presentation will look great for your seasonal party, and you'll be wishing you made more mistakes like this one in the kitchen.

I suggest Asian pears here because of the beautiful red and dark chocolate colors reminiscent of a traditional candy apple. However, any of the green and beige pear varieties that grow in Louisiana are wonderful with this recipe as well. For my seasonal produce list, see the resources index in the back of this book.

Special equipment needed: candy thermometer.

1 (12-ounce) bag dark chocolate

2 tablespoons heavy cream

12 Asian pears

1 cup chopped pecans

1   Add chocolate to skillet with two tablespoons heavy cream. Melt chocolate down on the *warm* setting and do not let it get hot (preferably no hotter than 115F, so make sure to monitor temperature with your candy thermometer). Chocolate should never go above this temperature, as it will begin to release an oily fat layer that just won't do. So, spare yourself the misery, be patient, and melt the chocolate on a medium-low setting, whisking the entire time.

2   When chocolate is fully melted, keep stove at this heat and slowly dip your Asian pears into the chocolate turning them in circular rounds until their bottoms are covered. Transfer to a bowl of chopped pecans, then wax paper (setting pears upright), and repeat until all of your pears are covered in the desired amount of nuts.

3   Refrigerate pears for 30 minutes and serve. Makes 6–12 servings.

Poached Pears with Mint

YOU MAY REALIZE that there's nothing I like to serve more during the fall Louisiana months than fresh ripe pears. As an appetizer, a dessert, or a topping to a salad, pears add a seasonal flavor to just about any dish.

For a dessert version of pears that offers subtle elegance at the end of any fall meal, try these simple Poached Pears with Mint. Poaching may be one of the most rewarding ways to prepare this fruit. By simmering pears in an easy simple syrup, the flavors of fall stay trapped under the fruit's skin until peeling. Underneath lies a soft yet firm dessert that's packed with natural flavor and elegance. Plate pears with ice cream and sprinkle with chopped mint for one jewel of a dessert.

4 pears

2 cups simmering water

juice and zest of one lemon

1 cup sugar

2 cups cold water

½ cup mint, finely chopped with extra leaves for garnishing

1 tablespoon almond extract

1 tablespoon vanilla extract

1   Score bottom of pears and set aside. Bring two cups water to a simmer, add lemon juice and lemon zest, and whisk in 1 cup sugar until dissolved.

2   Add 2 cups cold water, ¼ cup chopped mint, and extracts. Bring mixture to a boil. Reduce heat to a simmer and add pears so they stand up straight. Cover and simmer pears for 8–10 minutes or until tender.

3   Turn off heat and let pears sit for 30 minutes in syrup until ready to serve. Peel pears from bottom up, starting with their score marks. Bed fruit on remaining ¼ cup mint. Drizzle plates with poaching liquid and sprinkle with whole mint leaves. Serve pears by themselves or with vanilla or chocolate ice cream. Makes 4 servings.

Chocolate Cake with Red Wine Pears

BECAUSE PEAR DISHES are so easily addictive each fall, my take on a heavier, slightly more decadent use of Asian pears will please any fan of red wine. Instead of using the pear as the main ingredient in your final course, substitute a richly flavorful dark chocolate cake and use the pears as a substitute for simple icing. Instead of poaching pears in a simple syrup, use 2 cups full-bodied merlot (or other red wine) to infuse a tempting boozy take on poached pears. This substitution cuts calories while adding freshness to the final portion of any meal.

CAKE

1½ teaspoons salt

¾ teaspoon baking powder

3 cups all-purpose flour

1½ teaspoons baking soda

1 cup + 2 tablespoons canola (or vegetable) oil

1 cup + 2 tablespoons water

4 extra-large or 5 large eggs

¾ cup water

2–3 tablespoons almond extract

1 tablespoon vanilla extract, optional

2⅔ cups sugar

1 cup + 2 tablespoons cocoa, unsweetened

1   Prepare chocolate cake: Preheat oven to 350F. Spray down Bundt pan with nonstick spray. Set aside.

2   Sift dry ingredients: Salt, baking powder, flour, and baking soda. Set aside.

3   Create the wet mixture with a canola (or vegetable) oil and water base. Mix equal parts oil and water in a Kitchenaid mixer for 2 minutes.

4   Once oil and water have been mixing for 2–3 minutes, add eggs, ¾ cup water, almond (and vanilla if using) extract. Mix combination on low-medium for 1–2 minutes until fully integrated.

5   Add sugar and cocoa and mix until integrated making sure to scrape down the edges of your bowl.

6   *Slowly* add dry ingredients until fully integrated, making sure to scrape down the sides during the mixing process so that all of your dry ingredients and wet ingredients mix properly.

7   Pour batter evenly into Bundt pan and shake to smooth. Bake for 45 minutes, or until a knife comes out clean. Transfer to cooling rack and cool.

POACHED PEARS

4 pears

2 cups simmering water

2 cups full-bodied red wine such as merlot

1 cup sugar

2 cups cold water

1 tablespoon almond extract

1 tablespoon vanilla extract

8 Poach pears in red wine: Score bottom of pears and set aside. Bring 2 cups water to a simmer, add red wine, and whisk in 1 cup sugar until dissolved.

9 Add 2 cups cold water and extracts. Bring mixture to a boil. Reduce heat to a simmer and add pears so they stand up straight. Cover and simmer pears for 8–10 minutes or until tender.

10 Let pears sit for 30 minutes in syrup until ready to serve. Peel pears from bottom up starting with their score marks and bed on chocolate cake. Drizzle plates with red wine poaching liquid and sprinkle with powdered sugar and serve. Makes 4 servings.

Pumpkin Spice Bread Pudding

ONE OF MY earliest memories learning about cooking from my mom took place in front of our TV set. A rotund, white-haired New Orleans chef was preparing bread pudding, and my mom was watching him with intense concentration. Since she had spent several years cooking professionally in New Orleans, her interest in the dish encompassed a certain attentiveness I'd rarely ever seen on her face. Not knowing what the dessert was, I remember asking tons of questions as I tried to wrap my brain around a *pudding* made from *bread*.

Although this memory has grown increasingly fuzzy, I know for a fact it was the first time I'd ever heard of bread pudding and discovered a quintessential New Orleans dish. For my mom, bread pudding represented a fulfilling time in her youth cooking in a professional kitchen, and for me, it represented some culinary possibility I would one day beg her to try. Years later, I make my own bread pudding from homemade sweet bread based on the season it is prepared. New Orleans restaurants serve some of the best bread puddings in the world. Pumpkin being a seasonal variation that impresses dinner guests, the key to an impressive bread pudding is high-quality ingredients: don't use just any bread for the pudding, but make your own simple pumpkin sweetbread for a dish that really has the power to "wow." I like this pumpkin bread so much that I often eat it by itself.

Each fall, I use my favorite pumpkin bread recipe made even better by the transformation of the dessert into a decadent New Orleans–style pudding. Certainly, this recipe represents a fresh take on a New Orleans favorite, but it still evokes for me all the early nostalgia of learning about New Orleans cooking alongside my mom.

PUMPKIN SPICE GINGERBREAD

⅓ cup melted butter

¼ cup water

1 cup pumpkin puree

½–1 teaspoon nutmeg

½–1 teaspoon cinnamon

½–1 teaspoon allspice

½–1 teaspoon ground ginger

1 teaspoon vanilla extract (can add more)

2 eggs, beaten

1 cup sugar

½ teaspoon salt

1 teaspoon baking soda

1½ cups flour

1 cup pecans, chopped

SAUCE

1½ cup whole milk

1½ cup heavy cream

1 tablespoon almond extract

¼ cup sugar

¼ cup brown sugar

¼ cup maple syrup

1 can pumpkin puree

5 large egg yolks

2 tablespoons good-quality rum

1 Prepare pumpkin spice gingerbread: Preheat oven to 350F. Melt butter and add to a Kitchenaid mixer with ¼ cup water. Add pumpkin puree, mixing on low speed to combine.

2 Add spices—nutmeg, cinnamon, allspice, ginger, and vanilla. After spices are fully integrated, add beaten eggs and sugar. Add salt, baking soda, and flour, mixing until a thick batter forms.

3 Combine pecans with batter and pour into a well-greased Bundt pan or two small loaf pans. Bake for 45–55 minutes, or until a knife comes out clean. Remove from oven and cool before preparing the Pumpkin Bread Pudding.

4 Cut pumpkin bread into 1-inch cubes and spread across a large greased casserole dish. Toast cubes in oven for 15–20 minutes until lightly toasted on all sides (flip bread halfway through to toast other side). Remove from oven and cool.

5 Prepare Pumpkin Bread Pudding Sauce: In a large nonstick saucepan, combine milk, cream, and almond extract, whisking occasionally until simmering. In a separate bowl, create thickening egg mixture: Whisk together sugars, maple syrup, pumpkin puree, egg yolks, and rum.

6 Remove cream from heat and whisk pumpkin mixture with cream mixture until fully combined. Pour sauce over cooled toasted pumpkin bread cubes and set for 20 minutes to absorb sauce. I sometimes like to poke the bread with a toothpick to add pores that help soak up the sauce. Stir once or twice to ensure bread is fully coated.

7 Bake Pumpkin Bread Pudding for 40–45 minutes, or until a knife comes out clean. Remove from oven and cool for five minutes.

RUM SAUCE AND DRESSING

¼ cup dark brown sugar

¼ cup good-quality rum

1 teaspoon salt

1 teaspoon cinnamon

1 teaspoon allspice

powdered sugar, sifted

8 Prepare Rum Sauce: In a nonstick saucepan, whisk together brown sugar, rum, salt, and spices until simmering. Simmer for 3–5 minutes or until mixture has reduced by a fourth. Plate pumpkin bread pudding, drizzle with rum sauce, sprinkle with powdered sugar, and serve warm. Makes 8–10 servings.

Stuffed Baked Apples with Rum

ALTHOUGH APPLES ARE often associated with northern seasonal cooking this time of year, I find that southern cuisine has some of the best raw ingredients to fully actualize any apple dish: pecans, rum, and a bevy of southern spices. Together, North and South manage to meet peacefully with a kind of alluring flavor of which the Puritans surely never dreamed.

I love the juicy texture of baked apples with sugar, nuts, and rum. The servings are easy to dish out as each person gets their own apple, and the dish tastes much like a crustless apple pie. Once you've exhausted several ways to serve dessert pears on your seasonal menu, try this equally as an easy baked apple recipe with southern spices and rum.

⅓ cup brown sugar, packed

⅓ cup pecans (can substitute Bourbon Candied Pecans from Winter Appetizer section)

1 teaspoon cinnamon

1 teaspoon nutmeg

4 apples such as Granny Smith or Gala

2 tablespoons salted butter

RUM SAUCE

¼ cup dark brown sugar

¼ cup good-quality rum

1 teaspoon salt

1 teaspoon cinnamon

1 teaspoon allspice

1   Preheat oven to 350F. In a large bowl, whisk together sugar, pecans, cinnamon, and nutmeg. Set aside.

2   Core apples, using a sharp paring knife or apple corer. Place apples snugly inside individually greased muffin tins and pack each core with the sugar-and-spice mixture. Top each apple with ½ tablespoon butter.

3   Bake for 50 minutes to an hour or until apples are tender and bubbly. Remove from oven and cool for *at least* 5 minutes before serving (they will be *very hot!*).

4   Right before serving apples, prepare Rum Sauce: In a nonstick saucepan, whisk together brown sugar, rum, salt, and spices until simmering. Simmer for 3–5 minutes or until mixture has reduced by a fourth. Plate apples and drizzle with rum sauce. Makes 4 servings.

Don't have a muffin pan large enough to hold an individual apple? Place apples closely together (but not touching) in a casserole dish. Baked apple skins sometimes stick together after a slow roast and the addition of sugar can make for an even stickier situation.

Boudin, Sundried Tomato, and Spinach Omelet

SOMETIMES THE MOST simple, everyday dishes are secretly complex works of art, albeit "culinarily." Take omelets for example. Omelets are one of the most versatile, impressionable breakfast foods that we cook—they can be flavored for every palette—but are frequently the most ill prepared.

Why? Well, perhaps it's because it's all too easy to create a slapped-together job and call it "une omelette." Throw some scrambled eggs in a pan, fill it with whatever ingredients you have, and then flip the dish in half when the egg is done, yes?

Well . . . sort of. The fact is making an omelet the right way is a bit of a work of art. The pan must be just the right temperature (pretty hot so that you can cook the dish quickly) and the ingredients should be pre-cooked, not cooked alongside the eggs as cooking times vary for eggs and their filling ingredients. Getting your timing right leads to an egg that is well-done but seemingly fluffy, and a cheesy filling that is warm and flavorful.

Because there is an art to omelet making, read over the following ingredients and instructions slowly for the how-to on a perfect omelet. Special equipment needed: a skillet meant for an omelet or else a specific "omelet pan."

olive oil to coat pan

¼ cup spinach, washed and set aside

¼ cup sundried tomatoes, chopped

½ link Boudin, cut into pieces

salt and pepper, to taste

2 eggs, beaten

¼ cup cheese, shredded (I use sharp)

1 Prepare all ingredients ahead of time and set aside to reserve. Warm a small skillet (one typically meant for an omelet) and add a tablespoon of olive oil. Warm oil (about 1 minute on medium-high).

2 Add spinach, sundried tomatoes, and Boudin. Turn to coat in the olive oil and season lightly with salt and pepper. Cook down mixture for 2–3 minutes over medium heat.

3 Pour beaten eggs over spinach and sundried tomatoes. Cook for 1 minute.

4 Using your spatula, push the sides of the omelet toward the inside and tilt the pan so that any uncooked egg runs to the now exposed part of the pan. Repeat all around the pan so that you cook as much egg as possible. Cook for 30 seconds to 1 minute, or until egg is mostly done.

5 Sprinkle with more salt and pepper and cheese. Lift one half of omelet up and press down against the other half of the omelet, cooking for an additional 30 seconds. Remove from heat and plate and serve warm. Makes 1 serving.

Cheesy Southern Biscuits

BECOMING A SOUTHERN cook means having a staple biscuit recipe that never fails you. My father's mother used to make fabulous biscuits when I was a little girl that I loved to pull apart and smear with butter. Although I never had a chance to learn the recipe from her, I like to think this cheesy version reinvents the buttery flakiness of her perfect batches with a rustic fall twist.

Recipes for traditional southern biscuits seldom call for the inclusion of kosher salt. As a more modern take on a Louisiana favorite, I suggest sprinkling biscuits with kosher salt before cooking to add a subtle flavor to their buttery crusts.

2 cups flour, plus more for rolling

pinch kosher salt, plus more for sprinkling

2 teaspoons baking powder

8 tablespoons butter, cold and cut into tiny cubes

¾ cup buttermilk

2 green onions, finely chopped

½ cup Parmesan cheese

¼ cup cheddar cheese

shortening or butter for greasing baking sheet

1 Preheat oven to 375F. Combine dry ingredients in a large bowl—flour, salt, baking powder—and reserve.

2 Cut cold butter cubes into flour mixture until mixture begins to resemble a coarse meal. Slowly add in buttermilk, green onions, Parmesan, and cheddar, kneading until dough ball forms (do not overknead).

3 Roll dough out onto a well-floured surface and cut out circular rounds for biscuits. Transfer biscuits to a well-greased baking sheet or Silpat mat (my grandmother always used shortening to grease her baking sheets, but you can certainly use butter). Sprinkle biscuits with kosher salt and bake for 10–15 minutes or until bottoms are golden and biscuits are cooked all the way through. Remove from oven and cool slightly before serving. Makes 12–14 biscuits.

Hot Spiced Cider with Rum

WITHOUT FAIL, MY girlfriends love Hot Spiced Cider with Rum on cool fall nights. The beverage is easy to make, especially when you have short notice about a friend's visit. I always keep a gallon of organic apple cider in my fridge during the months of October and November, knowing that it will inevitably get used for this recipe or another.

Although I like to make just about everything from scratch (when time allows), I find that some things are just as tasty with certain store-bought privileges like easy-to-use gallons of apple cider. Feeling decadent? Two of my favorite variations of this recipe include the addition of a shot of rum to each glass right before serving with whipped cream and cinnamon, or the use of cored whole apples as serving cups.

1 gallon store-bought apple cider

1 tablespoon cloves

1 tablespoon allspice

1 tablespoon cinnamon

1–2 cups high-quality rum, to taste or preference

whipped cream, to garnish

cinnamon sticks, to garnish

1   Pour gallon of cider into a large pot and bring to a light boil. Whisk in cloves, allspice, cinnamon, and rum. Cover and reduce heat to a simmer for 20 minutes or until mixture has reduced by one-fourth.

2   Ladle cider into thick heatproof glasses or cored whole apples. Top with whipped cream and a cinnamon stick and serve warm. Makes 10–12 servings.

Apple Ginger Ale Cocktail

ON THOSE FALL nights when hot beverages just won't do—because it's still a bit *hot* outside—you can use the leftover spiced rum cider from the previous recipe in a cooling cocktail for friends. This recipe offers the same timesaving perks of my Hot Spiced Cider with Rum, but the refreshing cool of classic ginger ale. Combining the ginger ale makes the beverage less boozy, so feel free to add a shot of rum per glass if you feel the need to dress up the alcohol level of your cocktails. Blend cider with bubbly ginger ale for an inspiriting cocktail that tastes like fall.

6 cups Hot Spiced Cider with Rum (previous recipe)

3 cups ginger ale

1 apple, thinly sliced whole

1. In a large pitcher, mix together refrigerated hot-spiced cider with three cups ginger ale. Pour over ice in cocktail glasses or mason jars. Dress each jar with a slice of apple. Makes 6 servings.

Cajun-Spiced Pumpkin Seeds

PUMPKIN SEEDS ARE hands down one of my favorite snacks: crunchy with a little bit of chewiness, salty, or sweet, they're an easy, low-fat yummy treat. Ever since I've moved to southern Louisiana, pumpkin seeds have just gotten better too—using Tony Chachere's Cajun Seasoning instead of regular salt, my pumpkin seeds have a somewhat Cajun flair unlike the ones my mother used to make.

Yet, my love for pumpkin seeds has not always been so. As a little kid, I used to look around my classroom at snack time and wonder, "Why do I always get stuck with the weird snacks? Everyone has chips, string cheese, mini-pizza kits, cookies, granola bars, and treats. And I? I have pumpkin seeds!" I would sigh half angrily with disappointment. These sighs would always lead to more wondering, "Why do I have to have the hippie-food while everyone else gets to eat *normal* food?!" And it was true: I did, in fact, eat "hippie-food" as a kid (although these dishes would one day be dubbed "organic," "natural," and "healthy"). I was probably the only kid who toted around sandwich bags filled with pumpkin seeds and peanut butter and jelly sandwiches on pumpernickel bread. The perks of having a serious cook as a mother always seemed to show up in my lunch bag.

The below recipe is extraordinarily versatile and can be made to taste. As a child, my mom would prepare pumpkin seeds in the oven with butter, garlic, and salt. For this recipe, I call for olive oil, garlic, and Tony Chachere's Cajun Seasoning—a blend of salt and Cajun spices.

The moral of my story? Pumpkin seeds are great, especially when prepared with the right spices—olive oil, garlic, Tony's, and Italian seasoning. So, for the adults who love this snack, feel free to indulge in this perfect fall-time favorite and enjoy a little bit of Cajun cooking mixed into a typically New England fall treat. But for your kids? They might just prefer granola bars.

1 batch of fresh pumpkin seeds, washed, and fibrous threads removed

1–2 tablespoons olive oil

1–2 tablespoons Tony Chachere's Cajun Seasoning

1–2 tablespoons Italian seasoning

2–3 garlic cloves, pressed or minced

1 Preheat oven to 350F. Wash pumpkin seeds and remove any fibrous pumpkin attached.

2 Add pumpkin seeds to a small baking pan and add olive oil, Tony Chachere's Cajun Seasoning, Italian seasoning, and garlic. Stir with your hands to combine and toss until seeds are fully coated with seasonings.

3 Bake in oven for 10 minutes and using a spatula, mix and toss. Bake for 5 more minutes and remove from oven.

4 Cool seeds, serve as snacks or as a simple seed crust to my Pumpkin-Encrusted Chicken Parmesan in the entrée recipes of this section. Makes multiple small snack-size servings.

winter

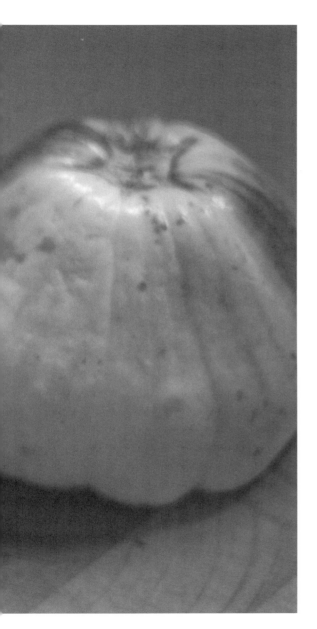

DECEMBER–FEBRUARY

At the end of the many hot days in Louisiana, colder ones produce the hardier vegetables and fruits I've waited for all year. Winter root vegetables in the form of hardy beets and Brussels sprouts create wonderful appetizers as with my Beets with Goat Cheese, Arugula, and Pecans (Appetizer) or my Brussels Sprouts with Butternut Squash and Pecans (Side Dish). Yet throughout this final section of *The Fresh Table,* there is an overwhelming sense that these recipes are authentic cold-weather items that blend the hotness of a meal with some seriously spicy ingredients. Beer-Steamed Clams, Spicy Cajun Bouillabaisse, Roast Duck à l'Orange, Beef Wellington, and Crawfish Potpie speak to the need for comfort food in cold months while embracing readily available citrus and garlic. Even wintertime desserts are a little warmer with my Hot Chocolate Azteca and its inclusion of fresh chili powder.

Beets with Goat Cheese, Arugula, and Pecans

Bourbon Candied Pecans

Pomegranate and Pistachio Crostini with
    Goat Cheese and Baguette

Baked Brie with Pomegranate

Swedish Meatballs with a Spicy Cajun Twist

Cleo's Oyster Artichoke Soup

Cleo's French Onion Soup

Beer-Steamed Clams with Crisp Bacon
    and Roasted Tomatoes

Individual Beef Wellingtons

Roast Duck with Orange Sauce

Crawfish Potpie

Cajun Bouillabaisse

Garlic Cheese Knots

Brussels Sprouts with Butternut Squash and Pecans

Bourbon Glazed Carrots

Warm Southern Corn Bread

White Chocolate Rocky Road

Chocolate Azteca Hot Chocolate [Spicy Hot Chocolate]

Pomegranate Christmas Cake with Snow-White
    Cream Cheese Icing

Orangettes: Dark-Chocolate-Covered Orange Peels

Coconut Date Balls

Wild Mushroom Onion Quiche

Holiday Eggnog

Holiday Pomtini Cocktail

Ciabatta Bread with Cheese, Garlic, and Herbs

Abita Molasses Beer Bread

APPETIZERS

Beets with Goat Cheese, Arugula, and Pecans

BEETS GET A bad rap. They're red, they mercilessly stain your teeth, and unless you're traveling in the northeastern United States, beets rarely appear on local menus.

But this doesn't mean that they aren't delicious despite their lack of geographical popularity in the South. A classic winter vegetable rich in nutrients such as potassium, folate, and yes, even vitamin C, beets are one of the easiest ways to bring a healthy, vibrantly colored spin to a simple salad. Beautifully plated with soft goat cheese and warm southern pecans, beets cozy up nicely to some of south Louisiana's most popular culinary ingredients any day.

For the easiest way to introduce beets into your diet, use the canned or jarred beets found at your local grocery store. Canned beets are quick additions for a cook with limited time and taste as good as fresh beets from the market (but without the messy cooking process). For those chefs with more time on their hands, see the cook's note at the end of this recipe for how to prepare fresh beets. In this recipe, soft goat cheese, crisp arugula, and warm pecans complement the earthy flavor of beets without shrouding it in toppings, but enriching the hardy sweet nature of this root vegetable.

2 (15-ounce) jars or cans sliced beets, drained, OR 1 pound fresh red beets

1 cup arugula

½ cup pecans

2 ounces goat cheese

1 Drain beets. Add to mixing bowl with arugula (measure based on personal preference) and pecans. Toss to combine.

2 Using a sharp knife, cut up goat cheese into small chunks and add to bowl and lightly fold into beet mixture and serve chilled or room temperature. Makes 6 servings.

When working with fresh beets, you will need to wash, roast, and fully cook the root before it can be cut into thin slices for this salad. To roast beets, turn oven to 400F and line a baking sheet with aluminum foil. Wash beetroots thoroughly and snip off green ends. Roast in oven for 1–2 hours or until tender to a fork. Remove from oven and cool to room temperature before peeling outer skin and slicing. Toss roasted beets with other ingredients.

Bourbon Candied Pecans

ONE OF THE most useful appetizers I make during the holidays will always be my spiced nuts. Inspired by the super-rich bourbon candied pecans I pick up at Fresh Market when I'm feeling that an expensive treat is in order, this homemade version is sweet, addictive, and ever so boozy. I've recreated my favorite keynote flavors here, but the key is to include white and brown sugar in the mixture to get that crunchy golden candy outer crust.

During the holidays, sugar and bourbon evoke my favorite seasonal flavors, and heaven forbid the bowl isn't completely empty at the end of your holiday party; of course you can always re-use the nuts for any recipe in this book that calls for pecans.

1 (6-ounce) bag pecans, shelled

6 tablespoons salted butter

⅓ cup brown sugar

⅓ cup sugar

1 teaspoon vanilla extract

1 tablespoon honey

⅓ cup bourbon

1. Preheat oven to 350F. Grease baking sheet and spread pecans evenly over it. Toast pecans for 3–5 minutes.

2. On the stovetop, melt down butter and whisk in brown and white sugar, vanilla, honey, and bourbon. Toss toasted pecans in glaze and simmer on low heat for about 5 minutes, or until mixture has reduced by one-fourth and pecans are thickly coated. Turn off heat and cool for 5 minutes.

3. On a clean surface lined with parchment paper, spread Bourbon Candied Pecans, keeping the pecans somewhat close together. Cool until candied pecans have hardened and break up. Toss with salads, desserts, or serve as a snack. Makes 10–12 servings.

Pomegranate and Pistachio Crostini
with Goat Cheese and Baguette

AS CHRISTMAS GETS closer, I become obsessed with the freshest ways to bring red and green to my table during the holiday season: rich goat cheese crostini topped in ruby red pomegranate seeds with warm and salty toasted pistachio nuts make for natural Christmas reds and greens. The combination is equal parts salty and sweet, red and green, fruity and nutty. I've always been a sucker for beautiful foods, especially ones that reinvent my favorite Christmas colors straight from nature itself.

These crostini wouldn't be complete without the addition of semisoft goat cheese. Although I realize that goat cheese is often an acquired taste, this tarter-than-average white cheese makes for a fantastic bed for sweet or salty items. Simply measure a 1:1 ratio of pomegranate seeds to pistachio nuts for a perfect balance of salty and sweet flavors on French bread. Feeling decadent? Toast the baguette slices in olive oil until golden brown before dressing in goat cheese, fruits, and nuts.

As the holidays grow closer, instead of reaching for your red and green food colorings, reach for deep reds and minty greens straight from nature itself with these Pomegranate Pistachio Crostini. They'll make you smile, and perhaps even taste a little bit like Christmas.

1 pomegranate, seeded

1 baguette, cut into 1-inch diagonal slices

5 ounces semisoft goat cheese

1 cup salted pistachios, shelled

2–3 tablespoons olive oil (optional, for toasting the bread if you choose to do so)

1 Seed pomegranate: Cut pomegranate in half and lightly pull seeds away from white tissue siding. I like to "massage" the seeds out instead of spooning or pulling them from the rind. This way, you rarely crush the berries and make use of the entire pomegranate.

2 Cut baguette into 1-inch diagonal slices and plate. Spread goat cheese over baguette and sprinkle with pomegranate seeds and pistachios. Serve and enjoy! Makes 8 servings.

For more information about working with pomegranate seeds, read "Cooking Methods, Techniques, and Food Preservation" at the beginning of this book.

Baked Brie with Pomegranate

WHENEVER I WANT to impress a new dinner guest, I always turn to this simple and decadent baked Brie. Cheese plates are holiday classics with wine and spirits, but a baked Brie in a pastry shell brings an impressive edge to your holiday table. I first encountered this dish with apples and pecans my first winter in Baton Rouge and have since come to love adding pomegranate seeds to my own variation. As for the pastry, I always advocate using store-bought puff pastries as they are a quick and easy way to wrap and bake your cheese in a flaky golden crust.

I suggest pomegranates here for a ruby red spin on holiday red, but baked Brie wheels can be prepared with any of your favorite seasonal fruits—spring strawberries, summer blueberries, fall apples, or winter pomegranates.

1 sheet puff pastry

1 Brie wheel, with or without rind

seeds of 1 pomegranate

¼ cup brown sugar

¼ cup maple syrup

1 Preheat oven to 350F. On a greased baking sheet, lay puff pastry flat after giving it ample time to thaw out. Place Brie wheel in center (with or without rind) and dress with one half of the pomegranate seeds. Wrap puff pastry over Brie wheel, pinch pastry edges together, and dress the top of the pastry with brown sugar and maple syrup.

2 Bake pastry for 25–30 minutes or until crust is golden brown. Remove from oven and cool for 5 minutes before serving. Dress puff pastry with the remaining pomegranate seeds around the perimeter of the Brie wheel and sprinkle a few on top with the maple syrup. Remove from oven and rest for several minutes before serving. Makes 8 servings.

Watermelon Juice with Basil, recipe on page 107

Fig and Prosciutto Salad with Goat Cheese and Spinach,
recipe on page 77

Avocado Egg Rolls with Honey Cilantro Asian Dipping
Sauce, recipe on page 74

Raspberry Almond Cream Cheese Tartlets,
recipe on page 98

Any-Season Crumble with Apricots and Almonds,
recipe on page 106

Above: Sundried Tomato Hummus, recipe on page 117

Below: BBQ Meatball Sliders, recipe on page 119

Pear and Pancetta Salad, recipe on page 122

Above: Tomato Basil Soup, recipe on page 125

Right: Sweet Potatoes with Goat Cheese and Bourbon
Candied Pecan Relish, recipe on page 138

Candied Pears (Dipped in Dark Chocolate and Chopped Pecans),
recipe on page 142

Brussels Sprouts with Butternut Squash and Pecans,
recipe on page 179

Above: Beer-Steamed Clams with Crisped Bacon and
Roasted Tomatoes, recipe on page 170

Left: Beets with Goat Cheese, Arugula, and Pecans,
recipe on page 161

Above: Pomegranate and Pistachio Crostini with Goat
Cheese and Baguette, recipe on page 163

Right: White Chocolate Rocky Road, recipe on page 182

Pomegranate Christmas Cake with Snow-White Cream Cheese Icing,
recipe on page 184

Swedish Meatballs with a Spicy Cajun Twist

FOR MY FINAL dedication to the sausage varieties at Marx Foods, I suggest an easy meatball recipe infused with Cajun spices. Marx prepares its sausages with everything from merlot to rare herbs, and I was most impressed by the way they used peppers to spice varieties of their sausage meat. Although Swedish meatballs are synonymous with rich gravies suffused with sour cream, I've included Cajun spices to bring life to this traditional base.

2 tablespoons olive oil, plus more to brown meatballs

4 cloves garlic, minced or pressed

½ onion, chopped fine

1 pound spicy turkey sausage

1 egg

¾ cup bread crumbs

1 tablespoon Worcestershire sauce

½ cup parsley, chopped fine

½ teaspoon allspice

½ teaspoon nutmeg

salt and pepper, to taste

1 tablespoon cayenne or chili powder

1 tablespoon Tony Chachere's Cajun Seasoning, or like Cajun seasoning

3 tablespoons flour

3 cups beef broth

1 tablespoon red jelly

¼ cup plain Greek yogurt or sour cream

1. In a large nonstick saucepan, add olive oil, garlic, and onion, sautéing over medium heat until onions are translucent—about 3–5 minutes. Remove from heat and bring to room temperature.

2. Prepare meatballs: In a large bowl, combine turkey, egg, breadcrumbs, Worcestershire sauce, spices, and sautéed onion mixture. Cover and refrigerate overnight to let spices flavor the meat.

3. When ready to cook meatballs, shape into 1-inch balls (mixture should yield anywhere from 16 to 20) and sauté in enough olive oil to coat the bottom of the pan lightly. Cover saucepan to seal in heat. Brown outside of the meatballs to ensure that they are cooked all the way through. Place cooked meatballs in a large serving dish and reserve while you make the sauce.

4. Retaining rendered juices from the sautéed meatballs, whisk flour with rendered sauce until a thick paste forms. Whisk in beef stock slowly and simmer until it reduces by one-fourth—about 10 minutes. Remove sauce from heat and stir in red jelly and Greek yogurt (or sour cream). Add meatballs to the pot, sprinkle with red cayenne or chili powder, and return to medium heat, simmering for 10 minutes. Serve with toothpicks and enjoy! Makes about 16–20 meatballs.

Cleo's Oyster Artichoke Soup

ONE OF THE most important recipes to me in this collection is, hands down, this Oyster Artichoke Soup. It's not just any soup. It's a soup rich in New Orleans history in more ways than one. How the recipe was acquired, where it was originally cooked, and how it was salvaged after Katrina gives voice to ways in which food and culture remain inseparable throughout Louisiana.

Allow me to explain.

"*That* is comfort food to me," Shannon, my hairdresser and good friend, says as she tells me about her favorite childhood recipes passed down from her grandmother. She's mentioning her grandmother Cleo and her Oyster Artichoke Soup.

These are the best recipes: family grown and nurtured, as flavorful as they are memorable.

When speaking with Shannon, I hadn't had this soup yet, but I could already see its perfection: fresh Gulf oysters promise the savory flavors of New Orleans seafood and quartered artichoke hearts promise the hardy richness of a truly complex, but delicious green. Cooked together, this classic pairing promises to be more than just a clearly delicious family recipe, but a clearly delicious recipe from a New Orleans family.

Shannon's memory of this dish is something akin to a Eudora Welty short story: set in the Deep South, filled with New Orleans characters, and ending in tragedy, the only remaining character is this soup. For Shannon's grandmother Cleo, food was an art. Although not a cook by profession (she worked at Maison Blanche in the wedding department on Canal Street), Cleo lived among some of the South's finest cooks. Because she didn't drive, or have a car, Cleo rode the bus to work every day. During her daily commute, she chatted up many of the chefs of four- and five-star restaurants, picking up tidbits for many of her recipes.

Now, Shannon's story would be fabulous if it just ended here, but it doesn't. In fact, like any great tale, it takes a bit of a turn. Cleo took cooking seriously and had a cabinet filled with cookbooks with handwritten recipes, notes, and ingredients. In 2005 during Hurricane Katrina, this cabinet was flooded, destroying all of the contents. Shannon was supposed to inherit these cookbooks and she tears up when she tells me this story.

Now being many years since Cleo rode the bus to Maison Blanche, many years since Maison Blanche even existed on Canal Street, many years since she last cooked, Cleo cannot recall the recipes or the notes from that cabinet.

Today, only two recipes exist, having survived Katrina: Cleo's Oyster Artichoke Soup and her French Onion Soup that follows this recipe.

As a resident of Louisiana, I take stories like this one seriously, recognizing that food in this state is always more complex than just the whisking of a roux or the spicing of a dish. And the thing that I find most fascinating about Shannon's experience is how it reminds me of the rebuilding efforts in the city. New Orleans is famous for surviving natural disasters and re-creating itself better than it was before. Now, every time Shannon makes this soup, I make this soup, or you, one of my readers, make this soup, I get the sense that we are all rebuilding a little bit of New Orleans.

Although this recipe follows the handwritten instructions Shannon gave me, there are several minor changes throughout: first, I bought pre-quartered artichoke hearts instead of the full-sized ones (which you would need to halve or quarter anyway); second, I used fresh canned oysters from Whole Foods instead of fresh-from-the-Gulf oysters; third, I added two cups of beef broth as indicated by the two cans. This soup is extremely rich, so the two cans added some necessary water where I saw fit. For instructions on how to shell Gulf oysters, see my recipe for Grilled Oysters with Bacon and Butter (Spring).

celery, to taste, chopped (optional)

1 medium-size onion, chopped

1 bell pepper, chopped

½ stick salted butter, or "oleo"

1 cup mushrooms, chopped,
optional

1 (10.5-ounce) can Campbell's Cream
of Mushroom Soup

1 (10.5-ounce) can Campbell's Cream
of Celery Soup

2–3 cups beef broth, enough to fill
the two empty cans of soup

whipping cream, to taste

2 (14-ounce) cans quartered
artichoke hearts

tarragon, to taste

rosemary, to taste

pepper, to taste

minced, or pressed garlic, to taste

salt and pepper ("black and white"),
to taste

2–3 dozen oysters fresh, or canned
fresh, 2 (8-ounce) cans

oyster juice (from oysters, or oyster
cans)

1   Dice Cleo's "Holy Trinity" into small chunks: Celery, onion, and bell pepper. Sauté holy trinity in oleo or butter. If using mushrooms, sauté with holy trinity. When onions are translucent, add cans of soup, two cans of beef broth, and whipping cream.

2   Let warm on low-medium heat. Cut artichokes into bite-size pieces (you can skip this step if using pre-quartered artichoke hearts) and add to soup. Add herbs, salt, and pepper. Taste. Add more if needed.

3   Add oysters and juice of oysters. Shannon writes, "if you aren't an oyster fan, you can chop up before putting into soup mixture."

4   Serve with crusty French bread and enjoy a little taste of Cleo's New Orleans. Makes 6–10 servings.

Cleo's French Onion Soup

FOR THOSE RARE cold stints in Louisiana weather, here's a second lovely soup from Shannon and her grandmother Cleo that will warm your winter body.

The great thing about French onion soup is that it's incredibly easy to make and requires very few ingredients. Combine warm beef broth with a ton of cooked Vidalia onions and you're halfway to making a bowl of soup. Literally.

I've made several revisions to Cleo's original recipe where I saw fit—primarily, I've cut down the excess butter and oil—but add additional butter or oil where absolutely necessary. For the warming taste of a New Orleans variation of French onion soup, try Cleo's below. It's easy and clearly delicious.

7 Vidalia onions (Cleo's recipe calls for 10)

1 stick salted butter

32 ounces beef broth (about 4–5 cups)

salt and pepper, to taste

provolone cheese, to garnish and broil

New Orleans French bread, for dipping

chives, to garnish

1   Chop onions "thick" and put aside. In the bottom of an oversized Dutch oven, melt salted butter and add onions. Cover and cook down until onions are tender and translucent.

2   Add beef broth and salt and pepper to onions and bring to a simmer. Allow beef and onion mixture to simmer for 30–45 minutes covered on medium to low heat.

3   Set oven to broil on high. Remove soup from heat and cover the top of the soup with thick New Orleans French bread and provolone cheese. Transfer pot to oven (uncovered) and broil until cheese is brown, golden, and bubbly (about 6–8 minutes, but oven times may vary). Remove from oven and serve with chives to garnish. Makes 8–10 servings.

ENTRÉES

Beer-Steamed Clams with Crisp Bacon
and Roasted Tomatoes

SINCE MY RECENT visit to the Gulf, I have wanted nothing more than to indulge in clams, fish, shrimp, and other delicious sea fare. Having found a small Asian food market on the outskirts of Baton Rouge that specializes in the most unexpected of seafood, I found fresh Louisiana clams without having to drive an hour to the coast.

Fresh is *always* best and for a quick and easy way to cook clams in your kitchen, try this delicious version of clams steamed in beer, crisp bacon, and roasted tomatoes. This recipe combines two of my favorite ingredients: Abita Amber and Louisiana clams. My recipe calls for clams to be steamed in beer with a combination of bacon and tomatoes to add flavor to the broth. It's easy, fast, and so clearly delicious. It'll warm any cold winter body with its light, hardy, delicious take on south Louisiana seafood.

2 strips bacon, diced (I prefer Maple Bacon)

½ onion, minced

1 clove garlic, pressed

1 teaspoon jalapeño, chopped fine

1 (12-ounce) bottle Abita Amber

2 pounds clams

1 (14.5-oz) can roasted tomatoes

1 lemon, quartered

1 tablespoon parsley, chopped fine

crusty bread

1 Rinse clams and transfer to a clean surface.

2 Add chopped bacon to a large pot and sauté until crispy. Add onion, garlic, and jalapeños. Sauté for 1–2 minutes until onions are tender.

3 Pour Abita into pot and heat until boiling lightly. Add clams and tomatoes. Spread clams around to even out. Cover pot and cook for 2–3 minutes. Check clams to see if they've opened. If clams still have not opened, cover and steam for 1 more minute. Discard any clams that are not open. Serve with lemon wedges, parsley, and crusty bread. Makes 3–4 servings.

Individual Beef Wellingtons

WHEN CLEARLY DELICIOUS was a food blogging baby, I made it a point to first cook those dishes I thought were most important for a food blogger (really, anything fancy and appropriate for dinner parties): Beef Wellington being my first experiment with culinary insanity (yes, I said "insanity," as the experience was trying and a bit expensive), but completely worth the effort. I had no idea when I started the cooking process that the final dish would taste like . . . well . . . *that.* Like the tenderest, most succulent meat I've ever tasted with the perfect combination of pastry, mushrooms, and tangy brown mustard.

I have since made this dish several times with increasing success and suggest it here in a smaller, more individualized form.

Many of my dinner guests have told me the beef to puff pastry ratio should be higher, and wrapping a cut of tenderloin in its own bed of pastry really satisfies these taste preferences. Plus, if it's your first time experimenting with this cut of meat, making it in smaller portions helps prevent the sabotaging of an expensive cut of meat with dreams of grandiosity. Whether you decide to serve the dish as a larger roast for a dinner party or as a romantic dinner for two, beef Wellington never disappoints.

Special equipment needed: meat thermometer.

2 tablespoons olive oil

1 pound beef tenderloin

salt and pepper, to taste

½ pound Portobello mushrooms, chopped fine

4 slices ham

2 tablespoons Dijon mustard

1 sheet pre-made puff pastry, thawed

1 egg yolk, beaten

1   Heat oil in a large nonstick saucepan and season your fillet with salt and pepper to taste. Sear fillet on all sides in saucepan until brown. Remove from pan and cool. Finely chop mushrooms.

2   Puree chopped mushrooms in a food processor or heavy-duty blender. Heat saucepan on medium-high heat. Cook mushrooms until they have released their juices and are tender. Once the moisture has cooked away from the mushrooms, remove pan from heat and cool.

3 Prepare the first stage of the Beef Wellington wrap: Lay two sheets of plastic wrap and cover with two slices of ham each so that your slices overlap. Spread mushrooms over the ham slices and put a beef fillet on top of each of these two layers. Brush Dijon mustard over the entire fillet and roll fillet in the ham and mushrooms, covering completely in the plastic wrap to seal your bundle tightly. Ensure that your plastic wrap is tight by using rubber bands to secure the ends, and refrigerate for 20 minutes. Remove puff pastries from the freezer and thaw for these 20–30 minutes.

4 Preheat oven to 400F. On a clean surface, lay puff pastry flat and halve (depending on the size of your store-bought pastry, you may need a second sheet of pastry dough). Unwrap both beef fillets and place each in the center of their own pastry dough. Beat 1 egg yolk and using a silicone brush, generously coat the edges of the pastry dough. Fold pastry around the beef fillet and cut off excess pastry.

5 Place Beef Wellingtons on greased baking sheet or Silpat mat *seam side down,* brush the top layer with your remaining egg mixture, and score incisions into the top of the pastry dough, but do not go all the way through the pastry.

6 Bake for 25–35 minutes. Pastry should be golden brown when removed from oven and meat temperature (yes, you should invest in a meat thermometer!) should be 125F–130F for medium-rare. Serve and enjoy! Makes a perfect dinner for two, but can be doubled for a dinner for four.

If pastry layers are more than two thick, you run the risk of their not cooking all of the way through and being doughy. Don't go crazy on the pastry here; one layer is enough for cooking purposes.

Roast Duck with Orange Sauce

DUCK À L'ORANGE has been a classic French dish served for years in many New Orleans bistros. Wintertime in Louisiana yields an impressive quantity of locally grown citrus produce, making it the perfect time of year to prepare any orange-infused dish. As winter brings on cooler weather, duck and citrus season arise at the same time. One of the many ways to use your oranges this season is in a full-bodied sweet orange sauce with roasted duck like this one. Naval oranges go best, but local citruses such as Satsumas from your garden will substitute nicely here for a unique Louisiana flavor.

Special equipment needed: meat thermometer.

DUCK

1 small bunch thyme, plus 2 tablespoons for rub

1 small bunch parsley, plus 2 tablespoons for rub

1 onion, chopped fine

1 tablespoon cinnamon

salt and pepper, to taste

1 (5-pound) duck

kosher salt, for tenderizing

3 oranges (can use Satsumas), 2 quartered and 1 squeezed for juice

½ celery, chopped fine

½ carrot, chopped fine

½ cup dry white wine

½ cup chicken stock

1. Preheat oven to 450F. Finely chop two tablespoons thyme and parsley, onion, carrot, and celery. Halve oranges. Set aside for preparing duck.

2. Prepare bird: In a bowl, combine two tablespoons thyme and parsley, one tablespoon cinnamon, and salt and pepper to taste. Pat duck dry and set on top of a roasting rack inside a roasting pan, making sure duck is breast-side down. Sprinkle duck with spice mixture inside and out. Rub duck with extra kosher salt to tenderize. Inside duck cavity, place orange wedges, half of the onion, and the bunches of parsley and thyme.

3. Surrounding the duck, spread the remaining onion, celery, and carrot. Roast duck for 35 minutes, reduce heat to 350F, and remove from oven for adding the wine.

4. Whisk together dry white wine with the juice of one orange. Pour wine mixture evenly over duck and return roasting pan to oven until a meat thermometer reads 170F at the thickest point in the bird (the thigh meat)—about 1 to 1½ hours.

ORANGE SAUCE

⅔ cup sugar

⅔ cup orange juice, freshly squeezed

½ teaspoon salt

6 tablespoons white-wine vinegar

6 tablespoons duck stock from the roasted duck

2 tablespoons butter

2 tablespoons flour

zest of 1 orange

5   When bird is cooked all the way through, carefully flip bird over onto its back so that it lies breast-side up in the roasting pan. Return bird to oven, heat broiler to high, and brown breast meat for 3–5 minutes or until dark golden brown.

6   Transfer duck to large cutting board to cool and carve. Pour pan juices (minus the vegetables) in a large saucepan to make the orange sauce.

7   Prepare orange sauce: In a large Dutch oven, cook sugar until it begins to caramelize and is golden brown, whisking occasionally. Reduce heat to low and add orange juice, salt, and white-wine vinegar until sugar is dissolved into a liquid.

8   In a separate saucepan, add butter and flour to duck stock, whisking until unified. Bring to a simmer and *slowly* whisk in orange mixture from Dutch oven. Whisk to combine and simmer sauce for 3–5 minutes. Transfer orange sauce to heat-safe serving dish such as gravy boat and top with the zest of 1 orange as a garnish. Serve orange sauce with roast duck. Makes 4–6 servings.

Crawfish Potpie

ONE OF THE perks of living in Louisiana is local chefs' region-specific take on potpie. Traditionally made with chicken or turkey, here this dish is a savory Cajun version of an American classic. Although this recipe can be prepared in a large pie pan, I love to make serving easy by filling ramekins with the filling and topping them with plenty of crusty pastry.

Special equipment needed: 6–8 oven-safe ramekins.

1 onion, chopped fine

½ green pepper, chopped fine

½ red pepper, chopped fine

1 celery stick, chopped fine

4 tablespoons parsley, chopped fine

1 box frozen puff pastry, thawed

1 stick salted butter, softened

2 garlic cloves, minced or pressed

½ cup flour

1 pound peeled crawfish tails

1 tablespoon cayenne or homemade chili powder

1 tablespoon Tony Chachere's Cajun Seasoning, or like Cajun seasoning

1 egg yolk

1 Preheat oven to 350F. Prepare ingredients: Chop onion, peppers, celery, and parsley. Set aside while you prepare crawfish filling. Roll out pre-made puff pastry, allowing for time to thaw while you prepare the crawfish filling.

2 Prepare crawfish filling on stovetop: Melt stick of butter, add garlic, and stir until fragrant (about 30 seconds). Whisk in flour and cook on medium until roux darkens to a golden brown. Add onion, peppers, and celery to pan, sautéing for 6–8 minutes or until vegetables are tender. Add crawfish tails, parsley, cayenne or chili powder, and Cajun seasoning. Cook for 2–3 minutes so that spices blend. Turn off heat and prepare individual potpies.

3 Prepare potpies: Line a sturdy baking sheet with ramekins and ladle crawfish mixture into each ramekin to three-fourths of the way full. Top each ramekin with 1 square of puff pastry and score tops with an "X" all the way through and brush with egg yolk. Bake potpies for 35–40 minutes, or until puff pastry is golden brown and filling is warm and bubbly. Remove from heat and rest for 3–5 minutes before serving. Makes 6–8.

Don't have ramekins? Use a standard 9-inch pie pan.

Cajun Bouillabaisse

"SO WHAT ARE you gonna make me?!" my friend "Uncle" Paul said last Christmas with his normal jovial stare. I often get this question from my family. Spending close to two hours thumbing through a variety of cookbooks, Paul and I went back-and-forth on recipes that every family member might enjoy. In traditional A.D.D. fashion, we jumped from *Monet's Table* to Fannie Farmer to *The New York Times* in search of the perfect—but seemingly easy—culinary treat. Then, we stumbled upon bouillabaisse. Scared I would have to make a dinner using chicken bones and other Depression-era concoctions, I came to the decision with Paul that yes, bouillabaisse was the dish we would be making with fresh seafood and no, he would not do much of the cooking.

I can explain bouillabaisse by giving an overview of its history. Bouillabaisse occupies a rich culinary tradition in France with a variety of opinions over how it can be made. Many French chefs argue that a proper bouillabaisse needs to have anywhere from five to seven different kinds of fish (not including shellfish), whereas others argue that a bouillabaisse can be made only if you live in the Marseilles region of France (from Nice to Menton), where they have an abundance of "ugly fish."

Having no ugly French fish on hand, I made—with Paul's humor and giving wallet—a bouillabaisse rich in New England seafood that I have adapted for the Gulf Coast here. Fresh shrimp, mussels, oysters, and fish simmered in a broth of roasted tomatoes, white wine, and clam juice that comforts with every bite. Cooked until warm, bubbly, and melted together with saffron, thyme, and fennel, this seafood soup is loaded with rich, flavorful seafood and depth.

For a Clearly Delicious treat for family or friends, try this fast and robust French bouillabaisse soup with Cajun spices. For the original New England variation, see available recipes at Clearly Delicious, which is listed in the online resources in the back of this book.

2 tablespoons parsley, chopped fine

1 teaspoon thyme, chopped fine

1 medium onion, chopped fine

1 stalk celery, chopped fine

1 leek, diced (removing woody ends)

3–5 cloves garlic, minced or pressed

¼ cup olive oil

2 bay leaves

2 cups crushed tomatoes

2 cups bottled clam juice

1½ cups dry white wine

salt and pepper to taste

pinch of saffron

¼ cup fennel, chopped, or ½ teaspoon crushed fennel seeds

Cajun seasoning, to taste

12 mussels, well scrubbed and de-bearded (can use more if available)

12–15 large raw shrimp, shelled and deveined

1 pound crawfish tails

1 pound red snapper or other local fish

12–15 scallops

1   Prepare ingredients: Chop parsley, thyme, onion, and celery; dice leek; and peel garlic for pressing or mincing.

2   In a large kettle heat the oil and add onion, celery, leek, thyme, bay leaf, and garlic. Cook down for 5–10 minutes or until vegetables are tender but still crisp.

3   Add tomatoes, clam juice, wine, salt, pepper, saffron, fennel, and Cajun seasoning such as Tony Chachere's Cajun Seasoning. Simmer for 15 minutes (if broth reduces too much, add more clam juice, wine, or water based on preference).

4   Add seafood in the order of cooking time: First add mussels and cover broth with a lid. Cook for 3–5 minutes, or until mussel shells have opened from steaming. Add shrimp, crawfish tails, and red snapper. Simmer for 3–5 more minutes and add scallops. Cook for 3 more minutes on a simmer. Serve with crusty bread. Makes 6–8 servings.

SIDE DISHES

Garlic Cheese Knots

FOR SOME REASON, bread just tastes better in winter. Perhaps it's the way crusty, freshly baked bread tastes in the cold weather, or perhaps it's the abundance of soups in my kitchen, but I find myself baking more than ever during the winter months. A staple side dish I love to cook alongside any meal is my Garlic Cheese Knots. Made with pre-prepared pizza dough, these garlic cheese knots take very little time to prepare while tasting ever so fresh with hardy winter herbs like rosemary and parsley. Paired alongside my Cajun Bouillabaisse or any other soup, Garlic Cheese Knots add a little comfort to winter cooking.

2 tablespoons parsley, chopped fine

1 teaspoon rosemary, chopped fine

2 cloves garlic, minced or pressed

1 batch pizza dough (see recipe in "Cooking Methods, Techniques, and Food Preservation")

flour, for rolling and dusting

½ cup Parmesan, more for sprinkling

kosher or sea salt and pepper, to taste

olive oil, for rolling

butter, for greasing baking sheet

1 Preheat oven to 350F; chop parsley and rosemary and mince garlic. Divide pizza dough into 8 pieces and roll each ball on a clean surface or cutting board sprinkled in flour, Parmesan, and garlic until you've formed a long rope a little longer than 7 or 8 inches. Tie dough into a knot. There are so many ways to form your knots—three bulbs or four bulbs—but I prefer a simple and easy knot in the dough (like you're knotting a shoe lace) and then tucking the ends under so that the knot sits on its ends on the baking sheet. Sprinkle knots with salt, pepper, parsley, rosemary, and remaining Parmesan. Drizzle with olive oil.

2 Evenly place knotted dough on a greased baking sheet or Silpat mat and rest for 15 minutes before baking in oven (this added time allows the dough to expand before going in the oven).

3 Bake for 15 minutes and check the doneness of the dough. Depending on oven size and temperature, you will need to continue baking the knots for an additional 5–10 minutes until golden brown. Remove from oven and serve immediately. Makes 8 garlic cheese knots.

Brussels Sprouts with Butternut Squash and Pecans

I WAS THE KID who always ate her vegetables. More specifically, I was the kid who always ate her Brussels sprouts. I know, I know, such children exist only in commercials with happy parents and Hidden Valley Ranch, but in truth, I love my Brussels sprouts. They're green, earthy, and taste great when roasted just right in salt and pepper. Add the warm green bulbs to a pan of bright butternut squash with roasted pecans, hazelnuts, or almonds and my mouth starts salivating just at the thought of it.

1 pound butternut squash

1 pound Brussels sprouts

salt and pepper to taste

1 teaspoon thyme

1 teaspoon sage

3 tablespoons olive oil

⅔ cup pecans

butter, to taste

1   Peel squash, remove seeds, and chop into 1-inch cubes. Add to mixing bowl.

2   Wash Brussels sprouts and combine with squash.

3   Toss squash and Brussels sprouts with salt, pepper, thyme, sage, and olive oil. Spread on a baking sheet. Preheat oven to 425F and roast for 20 minutes (or until vegetables are tender).

4   Toss cooked squash and Brussels sprouts with pecans and butter to taste. Makes 6–8 servings.

Looking to make this dish sweeter? Toss squash and Brussels sprouts with my Bourbon Candied Pecans recipe at the beginning of the winter section.

Bourbon Glazed Carrots

WHEN WE COOK for new dinner companions, there are certain side dishes that always go over well—mashed potatoes, macaroni and cheese, and sweet glazed carrots. Cooked with butter and sugar till tender but still firm, these winter root vegetables are almost like serving dessert with dinner. Prepared with a sinful touch of bourbon, roasted carrots make for a fabulous winter root vegetable and the bourbon glaze adds an exotic twist to an otherwise simple holiday classic.

1 pound baby carrots, washed

1 tablespoon parsley, chopped fine, plus more for garnish

2 tablespoons salted butter

½ cup brown sugar

1 clove garlic, minced or pressed

¼ cup bourbon

salt and pepper, to taste

cinnamon, for garnish

1   Wash carrots and chop parsley. Set aside.

2   Bring a medium-size pot of water to a boil and cook carrots covered until tender, about 15–20 minutes. Rinse and return carrots to pot.

3   While carrots are still hot, add butter, brown sugar, garlic, parsley, bourbon, and salt and pepper to taste. Mix ingredients to evenly coat carrots and transfer to serving dish. Sprinkle with cinnamon and parsley and serve warm. Makes 4–6 servings.

Warm Southern Corn Bread

THERE'S NOTHING I miss more during Louisiana winters than fresh summer corn. Although modern grocery stores make corn available to us all the year round, the crop just doesn't taste the same unless it's summer. For those of us yearning for summer in the dead of winter, revisit a favorite summer crop with an easy corn bread baked in a cast-iron skillet. This variation makes sure to sweeten an otherwise bland dish with the use of sugar inside a traditional southern cornbread recipe. Running low on time? Bake a store-bought box of corn bread mix according to manufacturer's instructions with the addition of shredded cheddar cheese.

Special equipment needed: 8- to 10-inch cast-iron skillet.

1 cup self-rising cornmeal

½ teaspoon baking soda

large pinch of salt

1½ cups shredded cheddar cheese

¾ cup sugar

1 garlic clove, minced or pressed

1 cup milk

2 eggs, beaten

1 Preheat oven to 350F and grease a cast-iron skillet. Set aside.

2 In a shallow bowl, whisk together dry ingredients—cornmeal, baking soda, salt, and cheddar cheese. Add in sugar and garlic, mixing to combine. Add wet ingredients—milk and eggs—and mix until batter forms. Scrape down sides, mix one last time, and pour batter into cast-iron skillet. Bake corn bread for 35–45 minutes, or until a toothpick comes out clean and crust is golden brown. Makes 6–8 servings.

White Chocolate Rocky Road

FOR SOME REASON, this White Chocolate Rocky Road always makes me think of Christmas. I may never understand why—it doesn't involve any of the peppermint or gingerbread flavors we seasonal cooks expect—but it does seem like Christmas with its snow-white landscape and candy bits. Or perhaps it's the fact that, just like a little kid, I want bright candy this time of year.

When filling your candy and cookie gift tins this season, try my unique spin on rocky road. Melted white chocolate creates bite-size pieces of candy filled with marshmallows, nuts, and gummy treats. Soon, I think you'll be wishing for this candy every Christmas.

This recipe is adapted from a candy confection I saw one Christmas online. For my first version at Clearly Delicious, see the electronic resources at the back of this book. Special equipment needed: candy thermometer.

2 cups white (bar) chocolate (high quality), chopped roughly

1 tablespoon whole milk

¼ cup salted pistachios, chopped roughly

¼ cup macadamias, chopped roughly

¾ cup colored marshmallows

½ cup gummy bears, chopped roughly

½ cup dried cranberries

1   Line a baking sheet with parchment paper and set aside. Roughly chop nuts and confectioneries and place in a glass bowl with cranberries.

2   Roughly chop white chocolate and melt down with milk in a microwave or in a small saucepan over medium heat (candy should not go above 115F; otherwise it will become increasingly greasy and be "ruined"). When white chocolate has melted, add to glass bowl and mix to combine with nuts, confectioneries, and cranberries.

3   Pour mixture onto parchment-lined cookie sheet and smooth to an even layer.

4   Refrigerate mixture (covered) overnight and cut into cube-like pieces to serve. Makes 12 bite-size servings.

Chocolate Azteca Hot Chocolate [Spicy Hot Chocolate]

ONE OF THE BENEFITS of being a food blogger (or really any food writer) has to be the little perks. Sure, after you're done cooking, that lovely dish awaits you, but the perks don't end there. In the twenty-first century, food bloggers have become part of an exciting trend—developing recipes for food enthusiasts and sampling new products. Many bloggers partner with specialty food companies to bring new dishes to their company's Web site and a whole sea of new readers to their blog.

Only on the Internet does such symbiosis work so perfectly! Of the many companies I've worked with and mentioned in this book, I must say one sticks out the most—Marx Foods. In 2011, I won the Marx's Foods Chile Recipe Development Challenge with my Chocolate Azteca Cupcakes. I was so intoxicated with the combination of dark chocolate and chilies that I couldn't help but make one more dish. This piping hot cup of Chocolate Azteca Hot Chocolate warms in surprising ways during the winter months. Bringing you the warming comfort of a traditional hot chocolate, it kicks into overdrive with the spicy warming aftertaste. For a new take on an old favorite, I suggest using those dried chilies from your summer garden for the spicy component. Or, head over to Marx Foods' Web site for their endless variety of spicy chilies.

2½ cups heavy cream

2½ cups milk (can use skim, but whole works best here)

1 teaspoon vanilla extract

⅛ cup cocoa powder

1–2 teaspoons chili powder from dried chilies (can use store-bought)

3 tablespoons honey

whipped cream and almonds, to garnish

This recipe asks for 1 to 2 teaspoons chili powder from dried chilies, but regular store-bought chili powder can easily be substituted. For the simple instructions on how to turn dried chilies into powder, see the instructional cooking techniques at the beginning of this book.

1   Add heavy cream, milk, vanilla, and cocoa powder to a medium saucepan. Warm over medium heat until mixture comes to a simmer. Reduce heat to low and allow the mixture to cook for 5–10 minutes or until the mixture is thick enough that it coats your stirring utensil. Make sure the brew does not boil over.

2   Add chili powder and honey to mixture, stirring continuously. Pour into 4 cups and top with whipped cream and almonds and serve hot. Makes 4 servings.

Pomegranate Christmas Cake
with Snow-White Cream Cheese Icing

ONE OF THE BEST parts about the holidays is the way in which traditions naturally evolve. One year, you make a fabulous coffee cake for the annual office party and then the next year it's become your token holiday treat, for every year that follows. For me, my holiday baking traditions started with a snow-white Christmas cake that I have no doubt I will be making until I'm 80. And then my children will be making until they're 80, and then their children . . . and in the hopes that the world doesn't end and you can still buy pomegranates, so will their children.

This snow-white vanilla cake incorporates a combination of cream cheese into a regular white icing and dresses itself in fresh ruby red pomegranates as an ever-so-decadent take on holiday cooking. It's as tasty as it is beautiful, and I just love how the red seeds glisten on the snow-white icing.

Try my recipe for a basic white cake this holiday season, but instead of adding colored icing designs, incorporate fresh pomegranate seeds between the iced layers of your cake and along the sides. Putting fresh pomegranate seeds on your Christmas cake? I just love starting new traditions.

CAKE

3½ cups all-purpose flour

6 teaspoons baking powder

1½ teaspoons salt

2½ cups sugar

1 cup unsalted butter (2 sticks), room temperature

1 teaspoon vanilla extract

1 teaspoon almond extract

1½ cups milk

9 egg whites

1   Preheat oven to 350F. Prepare batter: Mix flour, baking powder, and salt. Cream wet mixture—sugar, butter, vanilla and almond extract, milk, and egg whites. Slowly add dry mixture to wet one until the batter is fully incorporated, making sure to scrape down your bowl for any leftover dry ingredients.

2   Grease three baking sheets with butter and a good bit of flour to prevent the cake from sticking. Pour batter evenly between the three pans. Bake cakes for 25–30 minutes, or until a toothpick comes out clean. Remove cake from oven and cool completely.

ICING

3 sticks butter, softened

2 (8-ounce) packages cream cheese (regular, room temperature)

1 teaspoon vanilla extract

1 teaspoon almond extract

6 cups confectioner's sugar

seeds of 1 pomegranate, to garnish

vanilla fondant with green coloring, optional

3   Prepare icing: Cream butter, cream cheese, and vanilla and almond extracts with confectioner's sugar, making sure to add 1 cup confectioner's sugar at a time. I like to use the medium-fast speed on my Kitchenaid standing mixer so that all of the fat molecules incorporate smoothly.

4   Plate bottom layer of cake, ice with frosting, and sprinkle with a little less than one-third of your pomegranate seeds. Add layers two and three and repeat this step. When you get to the top layer, sprinkle pomegranate seeds around the sides of the cake and any choice decoration on top. For the green leaves pictured in this book, you may use any store-bought pre-made fondant, converting it to green with food coloring. I prefer a basic store-bought fondant available at any major specialty-cooking store (see electronic resources in the back of this book), but this ingredient can be found in the baking aisles of specialty food stores or online. Makes 12–15 very thick and tall slices.

Orangettes: Dark-Chocolate-Covered Orange Peels

LOUISIANA WINTERS ARE always made a little bit brighter by the abundance of locally grown Satsumas and citrus. A popular favorite, citrus pops up in early November at local farmers' markets and occupies trucks on the sides of the road well through Mardi Gras. This recipe is a fabulous way to use leftover orange peels that would normally be discarded. Use the orange peels from my Glazed Tarte Aux Baies in the Spring Desserts section, or from any other cooking project such as orange marmalade or citrus salsa.

Orange peels have a naturally lovely sweet quality that when candied and dipped in dark chocolate are straight from a child's storybook. Although I love the delicious juicy fruits by themselves, oranges are made even sweeter when candied. For an easy orange candy after you're done eating your fruit, try this Orangettes recipe.

Special equipment needed: candy thermometer.

3 cups orange peels (about 5 naval oranges), sliced into sticks

water, for blanching and simple syrup

1 cup sugar, for simple syrup

1 cup water, for simple syrup

16 ounces dark chocolate, for melting

2 tablespoons heavy cream

1   Peel oranges and cut skins into evenly shaped sticks (I prefer sticks that are about half an inch wide and as long as the rind).

2   Bring a medium-size pot of water to a boil and add the orange peels. Blanch for 3–5 minutes, drain, and repeat step one more time to remove any bitterness in the peels. Drain peels.

3   Bring sugar and water to a simmer and add drained orange peels. Reduce heat to simmer and set peels for 45 minutes to an hour, stirring occasionally. Drain orange peels on a wire rack and cool for 20 minutes.

4   When orange peels are cool, melt dark chocolate in heavy cream, whisking until melted. Keep heat on medium-low, being very cautious not to heat the chocolate above 115F (otherwise, it won't stick to the peels). Dip cooled peels in chocolate—either half of the peel or the entire peel—and return to wire rack to air dry and harden. Keep Orangettes refrigerated or in an airtight container. Makes 3 cups Orangettes.

Coconut Date Balls

"IS THAT HOW you eat?!" my close family friend Linda said while contorting her face in shock as she accentuated the word "eat?!"

I was savoring my first bite of her Coconut Date Balls for the first time in 10 years.

"Yes! Well . . . kind of. This is how I eat Coconut Date Balls!" I replied quickly (with Linda, you have to be *quick*).

The nutty ball batter with its melted butter, sugar, and chopped dates and nuts rolled in shaved coconut must be, hands down, the most delicious bite-size treat I have ever had. I just couldn't get enough of these date balls. Linda's batch yielded 22 (easily 24 if made a little smaller) and within one day of her making her first batch, I had eaten 12. Yes, 12. I am a grown woman, and I am not ashamed of this fact.

As any food writer will tell you, there are certain recipes that take you back to a specific time and place. Perhaps because scent and taste are so closely related with memory, or perhaps because a recipe is just so good it seals up everything you experience with it like some time capsule waiting to be unlocked. Linda's Coconut Date Balls unlock so many experiences for me: the first time I had them, my ten-year-old self devouring every date ball in our Christmas tin, and vivid memories of watching Linda make the balls each Christmas, getting her hands dirty and swearing like a French sailor.

These are my favorite memories associated with these date balls, but it wasn't until I was in my twenties that I discovered the even richer origins of this recipe. This treat doesn't come from some *Betty Crocker Cookbook,* or from some family recipe, but from a truly small publication by the Hope Volunteer Fire Department in Hope, Maine, circa 1986. Originally published to raise money for the Hope Volunteer Fire Department, the cookbook itself is a fascinating piece of small town publishing. Originally priced at $5.85 a copy in the 80s, and all proceeds went straight to the town.

My recipe for these Coconut Date Balls are more than just my favorite childhood treat, but part of a larger process of "tried and tested recipes . . . contributed by those wishing to help with the maintenance of the Hope Volunteer Fire Department." Memorable, Flavorful, and a Piece of Small Town Charity? Now that's Clearly Delicious!

This recipe is adapted from the 1986 Hope Fire Department Country Cookbook *(Hope, Maine), page 93. Although the book had a limited printing (probably 100 copies, give or take a few), the recipe is reprinted here courtesy of Linda's vast repertoire of local cookbooks. Originally, one Jessie Jacobs of Hope, Maine, submitted the recipe.*

½ cup butter

1 cup sugar

1 egg, beaten

1 cup dates (un-sugared, whole), cut up

2 cups Rice Krispies

½ cup pecans, chopped (original called for walnuts)

½ teaspoon vanilla extract

½ teaspoon almond extract

dash of salt

sugared shredded coconut, for rolling

If using chopped sugared dates, cut down the sugar to ¾ cup. This recipe assumes that you are using whole, un-sugared dates.

1   Add butter, sugar, egg, and dates on the stovetop. Melt down butter and sugar with egg and dates for five minutes on medium-low heat, stirring constantly. Cool mixture for one to two minutes.

2   Add Rice Krispies, pecans, extracts, and a dash of salt and mix to combine.

3   Using the wooden spoon with which you've been stirring the batter, scoop up the desired size of batter for your Coconut Date Balls. Usually, my balls are about the size of a golf ball, but you can spoon out batter to any size—larger or smaller—that you like. Scrape batter off spoon with a fork onto a coconut-covered surface. Using the fork, roll the ball until it is fully coated. Transfer ball to wax paper and repeat. Makes 22–24 balls (2 dozen).

Wild Mushroom Onion Quiche

I'VE DEVELOPED RECIPES before in which I herald my friend Lydia's love affair with quiche. I've photographed her making hungry faces at cooked quiche, I've made asparagus quiche with her present, and I've pretty much signed the secret seal of quiche family and friends. I am one with the quiche.

Wild mushrooms, although typically foraged in the fall, are best in winter. By the winter months they've been properly dried and sealed, ready for surprising recipes like this one. Louisiana is host to some of the country's more interesting varieties and whole forests like Kisatchie in central Louisiana have their own list of species. For the less adventurous seasonal cook, I suggest playing it safe with wild mushrooms from your local supermarket or an online distributor listed in the back of this book.

1 serving all-butter Pie Crust Recipe (see handling of pie dough and recipe in introductory materials)

1 cup chopped wild mushrooms

1 onion, chopped

2 tablespoons olive oil

3 eggs, beaten

½ cup milk

½ cup cream

1½ cups shredded cheese (I prefer half sharp cheddar and half Colby Jack)

salt and pepper, to taste

1 teaspoon thyme, chopped fine

1 teaspoon basil, chopped fine

1   Prepare pie crust ahead of time, following the technique outlined in "Cooking Methods, Techniques, and Food Preservation" at the beginning of this book. Preheat oven to 350F.

2   Slice mushrooms and chop onions. In a medium-size saucepan, heat olive oil over medium heat and add mushrooms and onion. Sauté until cooked completely (mushrooms will be tender and have rendered their juices and the onions will be translucent and brown).

3   Prepare filling: Add beaten eggs to milk and cream. Mix to combine with cheese.

4   Combine sautéed vegetables with egg mixture and mix together fully. Add spices and mix one last time. Pour in pie-crust-lined pie pan.

5   Cook for 25–35 minutes, or until a knife comes out clean and quiche is golden on top.

6   Remove from oven and rest for 5 minutes before eating. Makes 4–6 servings.

Holiday Eggnog

LIKE MY FALL cocktails with spiced cider, rum, or ginger ale, every season has that go-to cocktail you want to savor as you talk with friends. For the winter months, I always prepare a creamy homemade eggnog with bourbon or rum. This dish is my favorite nightcap on Christmas Eve, and a wonderful way to start a Christmas dinner.

The rule to a properly made eggnog comes down to the ratio of milk and eggs. For every 1 cup milk used, add 2 egg yolks.

4 egg yolks

½ cup sugar

2 cups milk

2 teaspoons clove

½ teaspoon nutmeg

1 teaspoon cinnamon, plus more for garnishing

1 teaspoon almond extract

1 teaspoon vanilla extract

½ cup bourbon or rum, optional

cinnamon sticks, to garnish

whipped cream, to garnish

1   Prepare egg-thickening mixture: In a standing Kitchenaid mixer, use whisk attachment to combine egg yolks and sugar until fluffy and pale yellow. Set aside while you prepare hot cream mixture.

2   Prepare hot cream mixture: Over medium-low heat, combine milk, spices—clove, nutmeg, and cinnamon—with almond and vanilla extracts. Turn up heat to medium and bring to a light boil about 6–10 minutes. Remove from heat.

3   Return Kitchenaid to low speed and *slowly* add hot milk to egg yolks, mixing until blend is fully incorporated. Pour new mixture back into saucepan and warm on medium heat, stirring occasionally until eggnog coats the back of a wooden spoon.

4   Add bourbon (or rum) and transfer to a covered saucepan, then to a refrigerator, and chill. Serve cold with cinnamon sticks, whipped cream, and more cinnamon to garnish. Makes 4–6 servings.

DO NOT let mixture boil, as it will curdle.

Holiday Pomtini Cocktail

THERE IS NO doubt this Holiday Pomtini Cocktail is the definitive girly drink. Like a Cosmopolitan, it combines pink fruit juice (part of it cranberry) with vodka, club soda, and lime juice. Although the base of the cocktail is seemingly Cosmopolitan, the addition of frozen pomegranate seeds act as time-released infusions (and ice cubes) for an elegant revision of a classic cocktail perfect for New Year. Looking to cut calories after a decadent winter holiday? I suggest skipping the simple syrup and using naturally sweet pomegranate and cranberry juice to liven your cocktail.

1 cup pomegranate juice

1 cup cranberry juice

juice from 1 lime, plus 2 limes quartered

2 cups vodka

club soda, for splashing

1 pomegranate, seeded and frozen in a sealed freezer bag

One cup pomegranate juice is an epic task for home chefs, but can easily be made with the use of a mortar and pestle. For instructions on how to make your own pomegranate juice, see Kitchen Tools and List of Equipment at the beginning of this book on how to use a mortar and pestle to crush seeds into a juice.

1   In a large pitcher, combine pomegranate juice, cranberry juice, lime juice, and vodka, stirring to combine.

2   Pour mixture into martini glasses and splash with club soda. Drop into each Pomtini frozen pomegranate seeds for natural ice cubes, garnish with quartered lime wedges, and serve chilled. Makes 4–6 servings.

Ciabatta Bread with Cheese, Garlic, and Herbs
(good for breakfast)

BREAD SHOULD BE eaten warm, crunchy on the outside, and yet soft on the inside. Perhaps I am a bread purist, but I truly believe that a good loaf of bread should always be fresh from the oven, have a perfect crust, and a soft, inviting inside.

But these demands constitute the bread of my dreams, only to be found at fancy French bistros, Italian bakeries, or some other magical place where food is an art and the bakers and I don't speak the same language.

But in a world where good things happen to good people, my bakery dreams have come true. And where did I find this bread? Italy? France? Not a chance. I have found the perfect loaf of basic white bread in my little kitchen in Baton Rouge. I don't know how it happened. It was so sudden, so unexpected, and then suddenly, a perfect loaf of bread.

Allow me to explain myself.

I was cooking my way through Jim Lahey's revolutionary book *My Bread* when I, too, had a revelation. Looking longingly at his perfect "Slipper Loaf," a Ciabatta bread from Italy, I thought, "I can make that! A simple white bread. Perhaps the inside of my bread will have the same holes and spongy texture." So, I went about combining my ingredients—the flour, the water, the yeast, and the salt. I kissed my covered bowl good night and woke up to the most beautiful dough ball I have ever seen. I was in love.

Quick to see if the dough ball would yield its revolutionary promise, I kneaded it and allowed it to rise for 2 more hours. Then, I cooked it in a preheated Dutch oven.

Voila! A golden loaf with a crackling crust and warm, inviting inside. I have made a perfect loaf of bread. Readers can make this loaf too without going to Italy or France. Just follow my lead with these basic ingredients, have patience, and follow the Dutch oven instructions *exactly*. You will not be disappointed. Your bread will be warm, crusty on the outside, and soft on the inside with this clearly delicious Ciabatta loaf.

This recipe has been adapted with cheese, garlic, and herbs from my favorite baker, Jim Lahey. For information on Jim's bakery, his book, and the no-knead method, see the online resources index in the back of this book. What's Jim's (and soon, your) secret? The slow-rise fermentation that brings European bakery bread into any Louisiana kitchen.

3 cups bread flour

1¼ teaspoons table salt

¼ teaspoon active, dry yeast

5 garlic cloves mashed, or pressed

2 tablespoons basil, chopped fine

2 tablespoons thyme, de-stemmed

2 tablespoons rosemary, de-stemmed

1½ cups cool water (55F–65F)

additional flour for dusting

1½ cups shredded cheddar cheese

1   Mix flour, salt, yeast, garlic, herbs, and water for 30 seconds. Cover mixture and let it sit overnight (12–18 hours).

2   When dough has risen for 12–18 hours, dust a surface with flour and roll dough ball onto floured surface. Knead cheese lightly and quickly into the dough ball. Do not overwork the dough or it will be tough and disappointing. Once ingredients are integrated and dough ball is coated in flour and dry to the touch, return to bowl, cover, and let it rise for two hours or until dough has doubled in size.

3   Thirty minutes before baking the bread, add your Dutch oven to a pre-heated 475F oven and preheat for 30 minutes. Remove Dutch oven from stove (be careful! the oven is hot!) and remove lid. Using a rubber spatula, or your hands, roll dough into the Dutch oven *carefully.* I prefer to cook with the dough ball seam-side up so that you get a nice crack across the top as it's cooking. Cover Dutch oven and return to stove. Cook for 30 minutes covered.

4   Remove Dutch oven from stove oven and remove lid from Dutch oven. The loaf should be golden brown. Return to oven and allow bread to cook uncovered for an additional 10–15 minutes until it has reached your desired golden brown coloring and is cooked all the way through. Remove bread and Dutch oven from stove and turn off heat. Using a metal spatula and well-covered hands and arms, transfer bread from Dutch oven to a bread rack or cutting board to stop the cooking process. Allow bread to cool for 10 minutes before carving (carving is easier when bread is still a little warm). Makes 10 slices of fresh bread.

Abita Molasses Beer Bread

IT SEEMS APPROPRIATE that the final recipe for this book would be an ode to Abita beer, one of the most popular Louisiana beverages any season. Easily one of my favorite alcohol-based ingredients since I moved to Louisiana, Abita has a complex flavor of hop and malt (especially the Abita Amber) that makes for some of the most aromatic cooking. Beer breads have a warm, sweet, and boozy quality that, when fresh from the oven, warms any cold hungry body. Serve alongside soups, stews, or by itself with butter for an easy sweetbread that's perfect for dinner or breakfast. Infuse a simple beer bread with this adult beverage for a taste of Louisiana flavor, freshly brewed here.

3 cups all-purpose flour

3¾ teaspoons baking powder

½ teaspoon salt

½ cup sugar

1 (12-ounce) bottle Abita Beer (I prefer Amber, Purple Haze, or a seasonal Christmas variety)

⅓ cup molasses or honey

1 Preheat oven to 350F. Grease a loaf pan and sprinkle with flour to prevent dough from sticking.

2 Prepare batter: Whisk together dry ingredients—flour, baking powder, salt, and sugar (although technically sugar is not considered a "dry" ingredient, it's considered "dry" here for our purposes). Add half of the beer bottle and mix to integrate with dry contents. Add molasses or honey, mix slightly, and add the last half of the beer until the dough comes together. Do not overmix.

3 Pour batter into loaf pan and bake until a knife comes out clean and the crust is golden brown—anywhere from 45 to 55 minutes. Remove from oven, cool slightly, and serve warm. Makes 12 servings.

Seasonal Calendar of Menus

SPRING

APPETIZER: Mango Salsa (23)

SALAD: Peeled Zucchini and Asparagus Salad with Spicy Wasabi (29)

ENTRÉE: Seared Ahi Tuna (35)

SIDE DISH: Roasted Red Potatoes with Rosemary (45)

DESSERT: Fruit Salad Bake with Curry (58)

LAGNIAPPE/BEVERAGE: Southern Mint Julep (65) or Absinthe, the New Orleans Way (63)

APPETIZER: Strawberry Brie Bruschetta (28)

SOUP: Velvety Asparagus Soup (31)

ENTRÉE: Bowtie Spinach Pesto Pasta with Wild Mushrooms (36)

SIDE DISH: Green Beans with Almonds (44)

DESSERT: Strawberry Pavlova with Chocolate (50)

LAGNIAPPE/BEVERAGE: Absinthe, the New Orleans Way (63)

APPETIZER: Spinach Artichoke Dip with Spicy Cayenne (27)

SALAD: Peeled Zucchini and Asparagus Salad with Spicy Wasabi (29)

ENTRÉE: Grilled Oysters with Bacon and Butter (38)

SIDE DISH: Stuffed Mushrooms (42)

DESSERT: Glazed Tarte aux Baies (French Berry Tart) (52)

LAGNIAPPE/BEVERAGE: Southern Mint Julep (65) or Absinthe, the New Orleans Way (63)

APPETIZER: Pea Pesto Crostini with Red Spring Onions, Shaved Parmesan, and Toasted Pine Nuts or with Sundried Tomatoes (26)

SALAD: Peeled Zucchini and Asparagus Salad with Spicy Wasabi (29)

ENTRÉE: Pizza Florentine (33)

SIDE DISH: Artichokes with Red Pepper Aioli (40)

DESSERT: Lemon Cake with Lemon Buttercream Icing (47)

LAGNIAPPE/BEVERAGE: Southern Mint Julep (65) or Absinthe, the New Orleans Way (63)

SUMMER

APPETIZER: Avocado Egg Rolls with Honey Cilantro Asian Dipping Sauce (74)

SALAD: Fig and Prosciutto Salad with Goat Cheese and Spinach (77)

ENTRÉE: Sirloin Steak with Herb Butter and (possibly) Egg (87)

SIDE DISH: Perfect Guacamole (89)

DESSERT: Blueberry Balsamic Gelato (100)

LAGNIAPPE/BEVERAGE: Lemonade with Variations—Pomegranate Lemonade, Strawberry Lemonade—or Limeade (111)

APPETIZER: Red and Yellow Bruschetta (71)

SALAD: Fig and Prosciutto Salad with Goat Cheese and Spinach (77)

ENTRÉE: Fig and Prosciutto Pizza (82)

SIDE DISH: Blistered Eggplant with Mozzarella (91)

DESSERT: Banana Pudding (104)

LAGNIAPPE/BEVERAGE: Watermelon Juice with Basil (107)

APPETIZER: Watermelon Radish Crostini with Butter and Sea Salt (73)

SOUP: Summer Gazpacho with Avocado and Cucumber (78)

ENTRÉE: Crawfish Étouffée Ravioli with Spicy Cream Sauce (79)

SIDE DISH: Pasta Salad with Zucchini, Almonds, and Goat Cheese (94)

DESSERT: Fruit Salad with Blood Orange Olive Oil and Blueberry Balsamic Dressing (96)

LAGNIAPPE/BEVERAGE: Watermelon Juice with Basil (107)

APPETIZER: Salsa Verde with Sweet Basil and Cilantro (72)

SALAD: Fig and Prosciutto Salad with Goat Cheese and Spinach (77)

ENTRÉE: Grilled Sausage Bedded with Blackened Summer Squash (84)

SIDE DISH: Smoked Salmon Carpaccio with Dill, Capers, and Quail Eggs (92)

DESSERT: Raspberry Almond Cream Cheese Tartlets (98)

LAGNIAPPE/BEVERAGE: Lemonade with Variations—Pomegranate Lemonade, Strawberry Lemonade—or Limeade (111)

AUTUMN

APPETIZER: Asian Pears with Honey, Gorgonzola, & Bourbon Candied Pecans (118)

SOUP: Rosemary's Rosemary Pumpkin Soup (123)

ENTRÉE: Pumpkin-Encrusted Chicken Parmesan (128)

SIDE DISH: Spiced Sweet Potatoes (134)

DESSERT: Stuffed Baked Apples with Rum (150)

LAGNIAPPE/BEVERAGE: Apple Ginger Ale Cocktail (155)

APPETIZER: BBQ Meatball Sliders (119)

SOUP: Tomato Basil Soup (125)

ENTRÉE: Michael's Mac and Blue Cheese (132)

SIDE DISH: Spaghetti Squash Roasted in Walnut Olive Oil, Garlic, and Parsley (136)

DESSERT: Candied Pears (Dipped in Dark Chocolate and Chopped Pecans) (142)

APPETIZER: Cheese-Stuffed Dates with Prosciutto (120)

ENTRÉE: Herbed Chicken with Pancetta Croissant Stuffing (126)

SIDE DISH: Cranberry Sauce (140)

DESSERT: Pumpkin Spice Bread Pudding (147)

LAGNIAPPE/BEVERAGE: Hot Spiced Cider with Rum (154)

APPETIZER: Easy Roasted Garlic with Thyme (121)
SOUP: Tomato Basil Soup (125)
ENTRÉE: Pumpkin Sage Ravioli (130)
SIDE DISH: Sweet Potatoes with Goat Cheese and Bourbon Candied Pecan Relish (138)
DESSERT: Chocolate Cake with Red Wine Pears (145)
LAGNIAPPE/BEVERAGE: Hot Spiced Cider with Rum (154)

WINTER

APPETIZER: Baked Brie with Pomegranate (164)
SOUP: Cleo's French Onion Soup (169)
ENTRÉE: Beer-Steamed Clams with Crisp Bacon and Roasted Tomatoes (170)
SIDE DISH: Bourbon Glazed Carrots (180)
DESSERT: Pomegranate Christmas Cake with Snow-White Cream Cheese Icing (184)
LAGNIAPPE/BEVERAGE: Holiday Eggnog (190) or Holiday Pomtini Cocktail (191)

APPETIZER: Beets with Goat Cheese, Arugula, and Pecans (161)
SOUP: Cleo's Oyster Artichoke Soup (166)
ENTRÉE: Crawfish Potpie (175)
SIDE DISH: Brussels Sprouts with Butternut Squash and Pecans (179)
DESSERT: Coconut Date Balls (187)
LAGNIAPPE/BEVERAGE: Holiday Eggnog (190) or Holiday Pomtini Cocktail (191)

APPETIZER: Bourbon Candied Pecans (162)
ENTRÉE: Cajun Bouillabaisse (176)
SIDE DISH: Warm Southern Corn Bread (181)
DESSERT: Orangettes: Dark-Chocolate-Covered Orange Peels (186)
LAGNIAPPE/BEVERAGE: Holiday Eggnog (190) or Holiday Pomtini Cocktail (191)

Produce Availability Chart

	JAN.	FEB.	MAR.	APRIL	MAY	JUNE	JULY	AUG.	SEP.	OCT.	NOV.	DEC.
Artichokes		×	×	×								
Arugula	×	×	×									
Asparagus		×	×	×	×	×						
Beets	×	×	×	×	×					×	×	×
Blackberries					×	×						
Blueberries					×	×						
Broccoli	×	×	×	×	×					×	×	×
Brussels Sprouts	×	×	×	×	×					×	×	×
Carrots	×	×	×	×	×					×	×	×
Celery	×	×		×	×						×	×
Corn					×	×	×					
Cucumbers					×	×	×	×	×	×	×	
Eggplant					×	×	×	×	×	×		
Figs						×	×	×	×	×		
Grapefruit	×	×	×									×
Grapes						×	×					
Lemons	×	×									×	×
Lettuce	×	×	×	×	×					×	×	×
Melons						×	×	×	×	×	×	
Mushrooms			×	×	×	×	×	×	×	×		

	JAN.	FEB.	MAR.	APRIL	MAY	JUNE	JULY	AUG.	SEP.	OCT.	NOV.	DEC.
Onions			×	×	×	×	×					
Oranges	×	×										×
Parsley	×	×	×	×	×					×	×	×
Peaches						×	×	×				
Pears						×	×	×				
Peas (English)				×	×							
Peas (Southern)						×	×	×	×	×		
Peppers (Bell)				×	×	×						
Peppers (Hot)				×	×	×	×	×	×	×		
Pomegranates						×	×	×	×	×	×	×
Pumpkins		×	×	×	×							
Radishes	×	×	×	×	×					×	×	×
Shallots	×	×	×	×	×					×	×	×
Spinach	×	×	×	×	×					×	×	×
Squash (Butternut)						×	×	×	×	×		
Squash (Summer)				×	×	×	×	×	×	×	×	
Strawberries		×	×	×	×							
Sweet Potatoes	×	×	×	×	×	×					×	×
Tomatoes						×	×	×	×	×	×	
Zucchini				×	×	×	×	×	×	×	×	

Source: Seasonal Schedule courtesy of LSU Ag Center at http://www.lsuagcenter.com

Reliable Online Resources
Web Sites Worth Visiting for Louisiana Ingredients, Recipes, and Overall Reading Pleasure

MUCH OF WHAT I do as a food writer takes place online. My blog, Clearly Delicious, and my column, "Fresh Ideas," accomplished with the Louisiana State newspaper *The Advocate*, represent a kind of growing trend with food writing and food photography: more and more, the most active and exciting conversations about food are taking place digitally.

To introduce readers to the kind of community to which I'm referring, here is a simple roll call of my favorite food blogs and cooking Web sites, food distributors, and other great places to get recipes, equipment, and concepts.

BLOGS

Bite and Booze—http://www.biteandbooze.com

Clearly Delicious—http://www.clearlydeliciousfoodblog.com

Cupcakes and Cashmere—http://www.cupcakesandcashmere.com

Foodgawker—http://www.foodgawker.com

Food Network—http://www.foodnetwork.com

Homemade Is Best—http://www.homemadeisbest.com

Louisiana Cookin'—http://www.louisianacookin.com

Simply Recipes—http://www.simplyrecipes.com

Smitten Kitchen—http://www.smittenkitchen.com

(A) Spicy Perspective—http://www.aspicyperspective.com

Sprinkle Bakes—http://www.sprinklebakes.com

Vanilla Garlic—http://wwwvanillagarlic.com

Steamy Kitchen—http://www.steamykitchen.com

WHERE TO FIND LOUISIANA INGREDIENTS, HERBS, AND SPECIALTY ITEMS

Cajun Grocer—online grocery store for authentic Cajun products, including fresh Louisiana Gulf shrimp, oysters, alligator, boiled crawfish, frog legs, and other specialty Louisiana foods at http://www.cajungrocer.com

Cajun Supermarket—online supermarket specializing in Cajun spices, ingredients, cookware, cookbooks, and other food items (Boudin, "turduchens," and more) at http://www.cajunsupermarket.com

Farm Fresh to You—resources for Community Supported Agriculture (CSA) for home shipping by local farmers in various parts of the country at http://www.farmfresh-toyou.com

Fioré Olive Oils and Vinegars—a Maine-based olive oil and vinegar company that offers different varieties of olive oils not available at Vom Fass: http://fioreoliveoils.com

Louisiana Crawfish Company—online crawfish shipping of cooked and live crawfish as well as king cakes at http://www.lacrawfish.com

Marx Foods—specialty foods, spices, and every ingredient you could possibly want or need, available at http://www.marxfoods.com

Randazzo's Camelia City Bakery—Best of New Orleans king cake bakery specializes in braided king cakes, pralines, fudge, gift baskets, and other New Orleans bakery-style custom orders with nationwide shipping at http://www.kingcakes.com

Red Stick Spice—Baton Rouge–based spice company at http://redstickspice.com

Sullivan Street Bakery, complete with recipes and information on the "no-knead method" inspired in some of the recipes in this book: http://www.sullivanstreet-bakery.com

Tony's Seafood—Baton Rouge–based Louisiana Gulf seafood company carrying prepared dishes, seafood of all kinds, cooking supplies, and more, with shipping available at http://www.tonyseafood.com

Vom Fass New Orleans—olive oils and vinegars: http://vomfassnola.com

Louisiana Farmers' Markets and Roadside Stands

Locations, dates, and other information courtesy of Louisiana Government's Farmers' Market Program. For more information on contacting sellers and on specific produce, visit http://www.ldaf.louisiana.gov

ACADIA PARISH
CHURCH POINT

Robert Matt–Roadside Stand
1557 Wikoff Cove Dr.
Year-round: 6:00 a.m.–6:00 p.m.

Robin Farms–Roadside Stand
317 Houston Richard Rd.
Year-round: Mon.–Fri. 10:00 a.m.–
6:00 p.m., Sat. 9:00 a.m.–2:00 p.m.

ALLEN PARISH
OBERLIN

Oberlin Farmers' Market
228 West 6th Avenue
Year-round: Wed. 9:00 a.m.–1:00 p.m.

REEVES

CM Farms–Roadside Stand
105 Vickers Ave.
Year-round: 8:00 a.m.–6:00 p.m.
(Non-summer hours vary.)

AVOYELLES PARISH
MARKSVILLE

Marksville's Farmers' Market
122 East Mark St.
Year-round: Sat. 8:00 a.m.–11:00 a.m.
(June; other months vary)

MOREAUVILLE

**Wesmar Farms Dairy Market–
   Roadside Stand**
851 Couvillion St.
Year-round: Thurs. 2:00 p.m.–
6:00 p.m.

BEAUREGARD PARISH
DERIDDER

Azalea Street Marketplace
Beauregard Parish Fairgrounds
(Exhibit Hall)
First weekend in every month
except October:
Fri. 12:00 p.m.–6:00 p.m.,
Sat. 9:00 a.m.–6:00 p.m., and
Sun. 9:00 a.m.–4:00 p.m.

Deridder Farmer's Market
206 North Washington Ave.
Year-round: 7:00 a.m.–5:00 p.m.

**Doherty's Tomato Patch & More!–
   Roadside Stand**
613 North Pine (Fairgrounds)
Seasonal: June–mid-Aug.

**E & B Produce and Nursery–
   Roadside Stand**
3570 Neal Oilfield Rd.
Year-round: Tues.–Sat. 9:00 a.m.–
6:00 p.m.

MERRYVILLE

**Merryville Fresh Produce Market–
   Roadside Stand**
11767 Hwy. 190 West
Seasonal: Mar.–Nov., 9:00 a.m.–
12:00 p.m.

BOSSIER PARISH
HAUGHTON

Blueberry Hill–Roadside Stand
5121 Bellevue Rd.
Seasonal: May–mid-July esp.,
Mon.–Sat. 6:00 a.m.–5:00 p.m.

CADDO PARISH

DIXIE

Ryan Farms–Roadside Stand
Seasonal: June–Aug., Mon.–Sat.
7:00 a.m.–5:00 p.m.; Oct.–early Dec.,
hours vary, call ahead

GREENWOOD

**Town of Greenwood's Farmers'
    Market**
William Peters Town Park
Seasonal: June–Aug.,
Sat. 8:00 a.m.–12:00 p.m.

SHREVEPORT

Dad-d's–Roadside Stand
Corner of Woolworth and Buncomb Rd.
Seasonal: June–Aug.,
Tues.–Fri. 8:00 a.m.–4:00 p.m.

JC Produce–Roadside Stand
Corner of Hwy. 1 and Martin Luther King
Seasonal: May–Sept.,
Tues.–Sat. 10:00 a.m.–4:00 p.m.

Matthew's Garden–Roadside Stand
8780 Buncombe Rd.
Seasonal: May–Nov.,
Mon.–Sat. 9:00 a.m.–6:00 p.m.

Shreveport Farmers' Market
101 Crockett St. (Festival Plaza)
Seasonal: June–Sept. and Oct.–Nov.,
days and hours vary

CALCASIEU PARISH

LAKE CHARLES

Charlestown Farmers' Market
Bilbo Street behind Old City Hall
Year-round: Sat. 8:00 a.m.–12:00 p.m.

**Doherty's Tomato Patch & More!–
    Roadside Stand**
Location 1: Corner of Sale/Nelson St.
Location 2: Hwy. 378 in Moss Bluff
(across from Sam Houston High
School)
Location 3: Hwy. 14 and Mcneese Rd.
at New Moon Driving Range
Seasonal: June–mid-Aug.,
Mon.–Sat. 9:00 a.m.–5:00 p.m.

CATAHOULA PARISH

JONESVILLE

Tolbert Produce–Roadside Stand
Seasonal: May–Oct.,
Mon.–Sat. 9:00 a.m.–5:00 p.m.

CONCORDIA PARISH

VIDALIA

**Plantation Pecan Co.–Roadside
    Stand**
1629 Carter St.
Seasonal: June–Aug.,
Wed. 2:00 p.m.–6:00 p.m.

DESOTO PARISH

GRAND CANE

Desoto Farmers' Market
10117 Hwy. 171 (Desoto Extension
Office)
Seasonal: May–June,
Sat. 7:30 a.m.–11:00 a.m.

EAST BATON ROUGE PARISH

BATON ROUGE

Red Stick Farmers Market #1
Corner of 5th and Main Streets
Year-round: Sat. 8:00 a.m.–12:00 p.m.

Red Stick Farmers Market #2
8470 Goodwood Blvd.
Seasonal: Apr.–early Dec.,
Tues. 8:00 a.m.–12:00 p.m.

Red Stick Farmers Market #3
6400 Perkins Rd.
Year-round: Thurs. 8:00 a.m.–12:00 p.m.

**Territo's Vegetable Stand–Roadside
    Stand**
7517 Highland Rd.
Seasonal: June–Aug.,
Mon.–Sat. 9:00 a.m.–5:30 p.m.,
Sun. 10:00 a.m.–5:00 p.m.

SLAUGHTER

Naquin's Farm–Roadside Stand
6351 Pride Port Hudson Rd.
Seasonal: May–Dec., 7 days/week
8:00 a.m.–6:00 p.m.

ZACHARY

Zachary Farmers' Market
Zachary City Hall, Main St.
Year-round: Sat. 8:00 a.m.–12:00 p.m.

EAST CARROLL PARISH

LAKE PROVIDENCE

Overby's Farm–Roadside Stand
408 Sparrow St.
Seasonal: June–Aug.,
Mon.–Sat. 6:00 a.m.–6:00 p.m.

T & T Produce–Roadside Stand
242 Travis Rd.
Seasonal: May–Sept.,
Mon.–Sat. 9:00 a.m.–6:00 p.m.

TRANSYLVANIA

Mom & Pop's Roadside Stand
14298 Hwy. 65 South
Seasonal: Apr.–Nov.,
Mon.–Sat. 8:00 a.m.–5:00 p.m.

EVANGELINE PARISH
VILLE PLATTE

Lee's Produce–Roadside Stand
4394 Opelousas Rd. (front of Crawfish
Center)
Seasonal: June–Nov.,
Wed. 8:00 a.m.–3:00 p.m.

Ville Platte Farmers' Market
704 North Soileau (Ville Platte
Northside Civic Center)
Seasonal: Late spring,
Fri. 5:00 p.m.–7:00 p.m.;
Late fall, days and hours vary

FRANKLIN PARISH
WINNSBORO

Henry Produce–Roadside Stand
451 Louisiana St.
Seasonal:May–Jan.,7:00a.m.–8:00p.m.

GRANT PARISH
POLLOCK

Robertson Produce–Roadside Stand
Hwy. 165
Seasonal: May–Nov.,
Mon.–Sat. 8:00 a.m.–5:00 p.m.

IBERIA PARISH
NEW IBERIA

Boutte's Shed–Roadside Stand
2113 Morning Glory
Seasonal: Months vary,
Mon.–Sat. 9:00 a.m.–5:00 p.m.

**Eddie Romero's Orchard–Roadside
    Stand**
5119 Freetown Rd.
Year-round: 7 days/week
8:00 a.m.–5:00 p.m.

Teche Area Farmers' Market
Main Street (Bouligny Plaza)
Year-round: Tues. 3:00 p.m.–6:00 p.m.,
Sat. 6:00 a.m.–10:00 a.m.

JEFFERSON PARISH
GRETNA

Gretna Farmers' Market
Huey P. Long Ave. (between 3rd and
4th Streets)
Year-round: Sat. 8:30 a.m.–12:30 p.m.

MARRERO

**Golden Harvest Produce #1–
    Roadside Stand**
1628 Barataria Blvd.
Year-round: Mon.–Sat.
9:00 a.m.–5:30 p.m.;
sometimes open Sunday

METAIRIE

**Golden Harvest Produce #2–
    Roadside Stand**
4309 Transcontinental
Year-round: Mon.–Sat.
9:00 a.m.–5:40 p.m.;
sometimes open Sunday

WESTWEGO

**Westwego Farmers & Fisheries
    Market**
484 Sala Ave. at 4th St.
Year-round: Sat. 8:30 a.m.–12:30 p.m.

JEFFERSON DAVIS PARISH
JENNINGS

Main Street Farmers' Market
Founders Park, Corner of Main St. &
Nezpique
Seasonal: Mid-May–Oct.,
Sat. 7:00 a.m.–9:00 a.m.

WELSH

Welsh Farmers' Market
201 South Elms St. (Welsh City Hall
Grounds)
Seasonal: May–Oct.,
Tues. 4:30 p.m.–6:30 p.m.

LAFAYETTE PARISH
LAFAYETTE

Acadiana Farmers' Market
801 Foreman Dr.
Year-round: Tues., Thurs., & Sat.
5:00 a.m.–10:00 a.m.

**Benson's Fresh Produce–Roadside
    Stand**
Corner of Ridge Road and Rue Der
Belier (Hwy. 93)
Seasonal: June–Aug.,
Mon.–Fri. 8:00 a.m.–6:00 p.m.,
Sat. 7:00 a.m.–12:00 p.m.

Lafayette Jockey Lot Flea Market
3011 N. W. Evangeline Trwy.
Year-round: Sat.–Sun.
8:00 a.m.–5:00 p.m.

LAFOURCHE PARISH
RACELAND

Diamond S Produce–Roadside Stand
2632 Highway 1
Seasonal: June–Nov.,
Tues. & Thurs. 1:00 p.m.–4:00 p.m.

THIBODAUX

Thibodaux Main Street Farmers' Market
314 St. Mary St.—Jean Lafitte National Historic Park
Seasonal: Spring (Apr.–July) and Fall (Sept.–Dec.),
Sat. 7:00 a.m.–11:00 a.m.

LASALLE PARISH

JENA

Farmers' Market Gardening & Gift Shop–Roadside Stand
3709 Hwy. 3104
Year-round: Mon.–Fri. 9:00 a.m.–5:00 p.m., Sat. 9:00 a.m.–12:00 p.m.

LINCOLN PARISH

CHOUDRANT

670 Walker Rd. (off Hwy. 80)
Seasonal: June–Sept.,
Mon.–Sat. 9:00 a.m.–5:00 p.m.

RUSTON

Mitcham Farms, LLC–Roadside Stand
1007 Woods Rd. (at Mitcham Orchard Rd. and Woods Rd.)
Seasonal: May–Aug.,
Mon.–Sat. 8:00 a.m.–5:00 p.m.

Ruston Farmers' Market
100th Block of Monroe St.
Seasonal: Apr.–Oct.,
Sat. 7:30 a.m.–11:30 a.m.

Yak's Produce–Roadside Stand
2800 Hwy. 167 South
Seasonal: Mid-May–mid-Sept.,
7 days/week 7:00 a.m.–6:00 p.m.

LIVINGSTON PARISH

DENHAM SPRINGS

Livingston Parish Farmers' Market
215 Florida St.
Year-round: 7:00 a.m.–12:00 p.m.

MADISON PARISH

TALLULAH

Grady's Garden–Roadside Stand
2621 Hwy. 65 South
Seasonal: June–Aug., 7 days/week
10:00 a.m.–5:00 p.m.

Tallulah Farmers' Market
404 North Cedar St. (Hwy. 65 North)
Seasonal: May–Aug., Oct.–Dec., Tues., Thurs., & Sat. 8:00 a.m.–12:00 p.m.

MOREHOUSE PARISH

BASTROP

Ferrell's Produce–Roadside Stand
5641 Shelton Cutoff Rd.
Seasonal: June–Sept.,
Mon.–Sat. 8:00 a.m.–5:00 p.m.

Main Street Market–Roadside Stand
224 North Washington St.
Seasonal: May–Nov.,
Mon.–Sat. 8:00 a.m.–5:00 p.m.

Morehouse Parish Farmers' Market
305 East Madison Avenue
Year-round: Mon.–Sat.
7:00 a.m.–5:00 p.m.

NATCHITOCHES PARISH

AJAX

Mims Produce–Roadside Stand
Intersection of Hwys. 487 & 174
Seasonal: May.–Nov.,
Mon.–Sat. 8:00 a.m.–5:30 p.m.

GOLDONNA

White's Farm–Roadside Stand
819 Hwy. 501
Seasonal: June–Aug.,
Mon.–Sat. 9:00 a.m.–6:00 p.m.

NATCHITOCHES

Cane River Green Market (Farmers' Market)
Downtown Riverbank, Natchitoches Historic District
Seasonal: Apr.–July, Oct. (select Saturdays), Sat. 8:00 a.m.–12:00 p.m.

ORLEANS PARISH

NEW ORLEANS

Crescent City Farmers' Market #1
Downtown—700 Magazine St. (at Girod St.)
Year-round: Sat. 8:00 a.m.–12:00 p.m.

Crescent City Farmers' Market #2
Uptown—200 Broadway (at the river)
Year-round: Tues. 9:00 a.m.–1:00 p.m.

Crescent City Farmers' Market #3
Mid-city—3700 Orleans Avenue (at the bayou)
Year-round: Thurs. 3:00 p.m.–7:00 p.m.

Marketplace at Armstrong Park
700–900 Block of North Rampart St. (in front of Armstrong Park)
Year-round (except Feb.):
Fri. 2:00 p.m.–5:00 p.m.

Our School at Blair Grocery–Roadside Stand
1740 Benton St. (in Lower Ninth Ward)
Year-round: Sun. 12:00 p.m.–4:00 p.m.

Sankofa Farmers' Market
5500 St. Claude Ave.
Year-round: Sat. 10:00 a.m.–2:00 p.m.

OUACHITA PARISH

CALHOUN

Thompson's Peach Farm–Roadside Stand
2195 Hwy. 144
Seasonal: May–Sept.,
Mon.–Sat. 8:00 a.m.–5:00 p.m.

MONROE

Matlock Farms–Roadside Stand
2733 Hwy. 594
Seasonal: June–Aug.,
Mon.–Sat. 7:00 a.m.–6:00 p.m.

Monroe Farmers' Market
1013 Washington St.
Seasonal: June–Aug.,
Mon.–Sat. 6:00 a.m.–1:00 p.m.

WEST MONROE

1700 North 7th St.
Year-round: Mon.–Sat.
8:00 a.m.–6:00 p.m.

PLAQUEMINES PARISH

BELLE CHASSE

Becnel's Farmers Market–Roadside Stand
9661 Hwy. 23 (across from entrance
to Belle Chasse Naval Air Station)
Year-round: 7 days/week
9:00 a.m.–6:00 p.m.

Ben & Ben Becnel's, Inc.–Roadside Stand
14977 Hwy. 23
Year-round: 7 days/week
8:00 a.m.–5:00 p.m.

George Brooks Farmers Market–Roadside Stand
14383 Hwy. 23
Seasonal: May–Jan., 7 days/week
8:00 a.m.–7:00 p.m.

POINTE COUPEE PARISH

BATCHELOR

Williams Produce–Roadside Stand
Turn west at caution light in Innis. Go
⅛ mile and look for sign on right.
Seasonal: May–Dec.,
Mon.–Fri. 4:00 p.m.–7:00 p.m.

NEW ROADS

Glaser's Produce Farm–Roadside Stand
8925 False River Rd.
Seasonal: Mar.–Dec.,
Mon.–Fri. 9:00 a.m.–5:00 p.m.

RAPIDES PARISH

ALEXANDRIA

Harris & Harris Produce–Roadside Stand
3705 Lee St.
Seasonal: May–Dec., Mon.–Tues.,
Fri.–Sat. 9:00 a.m.–5:00 p.m.

Ole Grey Mule–Roadside Stand
7835 Hwy. 71 South
Seasonal: May–Feb.,
Mon.–Sat. 9:30 a.m.–5:30 p.m.

BOYCE

Bayou Rapides Best Produce–Roadside Stand
196 Vercher Rd. (Hwy. 28 West)
Seasonal: May–Dec.,
Mon.–Fri. 8:00 a.m.–5:00 p.m.,
Sat. 8:00 a.m.–1:00 p.m.

CHENEYVILLE

Poole Produce–Roadside Stand
1621 Bayou Rd.
Seasonal: Mar.–Dec.,
7 days/week 8:00 a.m.–7:00 p.m.

FOREST HILL

Seasonal Sensations–Roadside Stand
11222 Hwy. 165 South
Seasonal: May–Nov.,
Mon.–Sat. 9:00 a.m.–5:00 p.m.

RED RIVER PARISH

COUSHATTA

858 Catfish Bend Rd.
Seasonal: May–Aug.,
Mon.–Sat. 8:00 a.m.–5:00 p.m.

Ed Lester Farms–Roadside Stand
1165 Hwy. 84 East
Seasonal: Mid-May–Aug.,
Mon.–Sat. 8:00 a.m.–5:30 p.m.

MARTIN

Me & D's Fruit Orchard–Roadside Stand
1263 Hwy. 787
Seasonal: May–Aug.,
7 days/week 8:00 a.m.–8:00 p.m.

RICHLAND PARISH

MANGHAM

Jones Produce–Roadside Stand
1213 Hwy. 622
Seasonal: June–Aug.,
Mon.–Sat. 7:00 a.m.–7:00 p.m.

RAYVILLE

Dehlco Produce–Roadside Stand
Corner of Julia and Blackmon Streets
Seasonal: Apr.–Dec., open when
produce available 8:00 a.m.–6:00 p.m.

**Richland Produce Plus–Roadside
Stand**
1811 Louisa St.
Year-round: Mon.–Sat. 8:00 a.m.–5:30
p.m., Sun. 11:00 a.m.–5:00 p.m.

ST. BERNARD PARISH

CHALMETTE

Johnny's Produce–Roadside Stand
601 East St. Bernard Hwy.
Seasonal: Mar.–Jan.,
Mon.–Sat. 8:00 a.m.–5:00 p.m.

ST. CHARLES PARISH

DESTREHAN

German Coast Farmers' Market #1
13786 River Rd.
Year-round: Sat. 8:00 a.m.–12:00 p.m.

LULING

German Coast Farmers' Market #2
12715 Hwy. 90 (St. Charles Plaza)
Year-round: Wed. 3:00 p.m.–6:00 p.m.

NEW SARPY

Schexnaydre Farm–Roadside Stand
Victoria Plantation on La. 48
Seasonal: May–Dec.,
Mon., Thurs. 12:00 p.m.–5:00 p.m.

TAFT

Zeringue Farms–Roadside Stand
16657 Hwy. 18
Seasonal: June–"End of Tomato
Season,"
7 days/week 10:00 a.m.–7:00 p.m.

ST. HELENA PARISH

GREENSBURG

**Ronnie & Rae Bardwell–Roadside
Stand**
766 Taylor St.
Seasonal: June–Nov.,
Mon.–Fri. 4:30 p.m.–6:30 p.m.

ST. JOHN PARISH

LAPLACE

Bailey's Produce–Roadside Stand
504 West Airline Hwy.
Seasonal: when produce available
Mon.–Sat. 10:00 a.m.–4:00 p.m.

ST. LANDRY PARISH

OPELOUSAS

**Fresh Picked Produce–Roadside
Stand**
1509 West Landry St.
Year-round: Mon.–Fri. 8:00 a.m.–5:00
p.m., Sat. 8:00 a.m.–3:00 p.m.

**Opelousas Lighthouse Mission–
Roadside Stand**
704 West South St.
Year-round: 7 days/week
7:00 a.m.–7:00 p.m.

St. Landry Parish Farmer's Market
Corner of Hwy. 190 and Academy St.
Seasonal: Apr.–Nov., Tues., Thurs., &
Sat. 6:30 a.m.–11:00 a.m.

WASHINGTON

Lee's Produce–Roadside Stand
Location 1: 193 Hwy. 363; Location 2:
310 North Main St.
Year-round: Hours and days vary

ST. MARTIN PARISH

BREAUX BRIDGE

1510 North Berard St.
Seasonal: Oct.–Feb.,
7 days/week 8:00 a.m.–5:00 p.m.

ST. MARY PARISH

FRANKLIN

Franklin Farmers' Market
306 Willow St.
Year-round: Sat. 8:00 a.m.–12:00 p.m.,
Tues. 2:00 p.m.–6:00 p.m.

Karen Allen–Roadside Stand
6460 Hwy. 317
Seasonal: Sun. 2:00 p.m.–5:00 p.m.

ST. TAMMANY PARISH

COVINGTON

Covington Farmers' Market #1
609 North Columbia St.
Year-round: Sat. 8:00 a.m.–12:00 p.m.

Covington Farmers' Market #2
419 North New Hampshire St.
Year-round: Wed. 10:00 a.m.–2:00 p.m.

MANDEVILLE

**Mandeville Trailhead Community
Market**
675 Lafitte St.
Year-round: Sat. 9:00 a.m.–1:00 p.m.

SLIDELL

Camelia City Farmers' Market
City Parking Lot at Robert St. & Front
St. (Olde Towne Slidell)
Year-round: Sat. 8:00 a.m.–12:00 p.m.

Rick's Produce–Roadside Stand
Hwy. 190 West (Gause Blvd. West—
halfway between Northshore Blvd.
and Hwy. 433)
Year-round: 7 days/week
9:00 a.m.–"Dark"

TANGIPAHOA PARISH
AMITE
Berry Best Produce–Roadside Stand
905 West Oak St.
Year-round: Mon.–Sat. 8:00 a.m.–6:00
p.m., Sun. 8:00 a.m.–2:00 p.m.

HAMMOND
Berry Town Express–Roadside Stand
923 South Morrison Blvd.
Year-round: Mon.–Sat. 8:00 a.m.–5:30
p.m.

Berry Town Produce–Roadside Stand
2600 West Church St.
Year-round: Mon.–Sat. 8:00 a.m.–6:00
p.m., Sun. 11:00 a.m.–5:00 p.m.

Deluxe Harvest–Roadside Stand
14065 Club Deluxe Rd.
Year-round: Mon.–Sat. 7:30 a.m.–5:00
p.m., Sun. 8:00 a.m.–12:00 p.m.

PONCHATOULA
Berry Town Produce–Roadside Stand
201 Southwest Railroad Ave.
Year-round: Mon.–Sat. 8:00 a.m.–5:30
p.m., Sun. 11:00 a.m.–5:00 p.m.

**Mary's Country Produce–Roadside
Stand**
21531 Hwy. 22
Year-round: Mon.–Sat. 10:00 a.m.–
6:00 p.m.

TENSAS PARISH
SAINT JOSEPH
**Harris & Harris Produce–Roadside
Stand**
157 Newton St.
Seasonal: May–Dec., Mon.–Tues.,
Fri.–Sat. 9:00 a.m.–5:00 p.m.

**Hopper's Produce Stand–Roadside
Stand**
118 Industrial Park Dr.
Seasonal: May–Aug., 7 days/week
8:00 a.m.–5:00 p.m.

WATERPROOF
**Plantation Pecan Co.–Roadside
Stand**
8642 Hwy. 65
Seasonal: May–Sept., Mon.–Sat. 8:00
a.m.–6:00 p.m.

TERREBONNE PARISH
HOUMA
Cajun Farmers' Market
Corner of Naquin St. & Martin L. King
Blvd.
Year-round: Mon.–Sat. 6:00 a.m.–6:00
p.m.

**Steve's Fresh Produce–Roadside
Stand**
4337 Bayou Side Dr.
Year-round: 7 days/week
8:00 a.m.–5:00 p.m.

UNION PARISH
FARMERVILLE
Yak's Produce–Roadside Stand
11246 Hwy. 33
Seasonal: Mid-May–mid-Sept.,
7 days/week 7:00 a.m.–6:00 p.m.

VERMILLION PARISH
ABBEVILLE
**Esther's Best Produce–Roadside
Stand**
12316 West La. Hwy. 82
Year-round: Fri. 12:00 p.m.–5:00 p.m.;
Mar.–Sept.,Thurs. 12:00 p.m.–5:00 pm.

GUEYDEN
Gueyden Farmers' Market
600 Main St.
Seasonal: June–Nov., 1st & 3rd Sat. of
month 8:00 a.m.–12:00 p.m.

VERNON PARISH
LEESVILLE
Third Street Market
500 Block of South Third St.
Seasonal: Apr.–Nov., Mon., Wed.,
Fri.–Sat. 7:00 a.m.–"Until Sold Out"

WEST CARROLL PARISH
KILBOURNE
Wanda Morehead–Roadside Stand
325 Franklin St.
Seasonal: July–Aug., 7 days/week
7:00 a.m.–6:00 p.m.

OAK GROVE
**Head's Produce Farm–Roadside
Stand**
8895 Hwy. 2
Seasonal: June–July, Sept.–Nov.,
Mon.–Sat. 7:00 a.m.–6:00 p.m.

Mayhall Farms–Roadside Stand
1826 Roundhill Rd.
Seasonal: May–Sept., 7 days/week
all day

PIONEER

Mack's Tomatoes & Produce–Roadside Stand
630 Cherry St.
Seasonal: May–Sept., 7 days/week
7:00 a.m.–7:00 p.m.

WEST FELICIANA PARISH
ST. FRANCISVILLE

Logan's Farms–Roadside Stand
7708 Hwy. 61
Seasonal: June–Nov.,
Mon.–Sat. 9:00 a.m.–4:00 p.m.

St. Francisville Farmers' Market
Fair Barn on Wilcox St.
Seasonal: Last Thurs. in May–1st
freeze, Thurs. 9:00 a.m.–1:00 p.m.

WINN PARISH
SALINE LAKE COMMUNITY

Leeper Produce–Roadside Stand
136 Key Hole Camp Rd.
Seasonal: May–Sept.,
Mon.–Fri. 8:00 a.m.–5:00 p.m.

WINNFIELD

F F & M Farms–Roadside Stand
1640 Hwy. 472
Seasonal: Oct.–Jan.,
Mon.–Sat. 1:00 p.m.–5:00 p.m.

Winn Farmers' Market
301 West Main St.
Seasonal: May–Aug.,
Tues. & Fri. 7:30 a.m.–11:30 a.m.

Recipes by the Book
A Regular Legend of Seasonal Recipes

APPETIZERS

Asian Pears with Honey, Gorgonzola, and Bourbon Candied Pecans (Autumn, 118)

Avocado Egg Rolls with Honey Cilantro Asian Dipping Sauce (Summer, 74)

Baked Brie with Pomegranate (Winter, 164)

Beets with Goat Cheese, Arugula, and Pecans (Winter, 161)

BBQ Meatball Sliders (Autumn, 119)

Black Bean Corn Salsa (Summer, 76)

Bourbon Candied Pecans (Winter, 162)

Cheese-Stuffed Dates with Prosciutto (Autumn, 120)

Easy Roasted Garlic with Thyme (Autumn, 121)

Mango Salsa (Spring, 23)

Pea Pesto Crostini with Red Spring Onions, Shaved Parmesan, and Toasted Pine Nuts (Spring, 26)

Pea Pesto Crostini with Sundried Tomatoes (Spring, 26)

Petite Crab Cakes with Cajun Dipping Sauce (Spring, 24)

Pomegranate and Pistachio Crostini with Goat Cheese and Baguette (Winter, 163)

Red and Yellow Bruschetta (Summer, 71)

Salsa Verde with Sweet Basil and Cilantro (Summer, 72)

Spinach Artichoke Dip with Spicy Cayenne (Spring, 27)

Strawberry Brie Bruschetta (Spring, 28)

Sundried Tomato Hummus (Autumn, 117)

Swedish Meatballs with a Spicy Cajun Twist (Winter, 165)

Watermelon Radish Crostini with Butter and Sea Salt (Summer, 73)

SOUPS AND SALADS

Antipasti Avocado Asparagus Salad (Spring, 30)

Cleo's French Onion Soup (Winter, 169)

Cleo's Oyster Artichoke Soup (Winter, 166)

Fig and Prosciutto Salad with Goat Cheese and Spinach (Summer, 77)

Pear and Pancetta Salad (Autumn, 122)

Peeled Zucchini and Asparagus Salad with Spicy Wasabi (Spring, 29)

Rosemary's Rosemary Pumpkin Soup (Autumn, 123)

Summer Gazpacho with Avocado and Cucumber (Summer, 78)

Tomato Basil Soup (Autumn, 125)

Velvety Asparagus Soup (Spring, 31)

ENTRÉES

Beer Can Chicken (Spring, 37)

Beef Wellingtons, Individual (Winter, 171)

Beer-Steamed Clams with Crisp Bacon and Roasted Tomatoes (Winter, 170)

Boudin Pizza (Summer, 82)

Bowtie Spinach Pesto Pasta with Wild Mushrooms (Spring, 36)

Cajun Bouillabaisse (Winter, 176)

Crawfish Étouffée Ravioli with Spicy Cream Sauce (Summer, 79)

Crawfish Potpie (Winter, 175)

Fig and Prosciutto Pizza (Summer, 82)

Grilled Oysters with Bacon and Butter (Spring, 38)

Grilled Sausage Bedded with Blackened Summer Squash (Summer, 84)

Herbed Chicken with Pancetta Croissant Stuffing (Autumn, 126)

Michael's Mac and Blue Cheese (Autumn, 132)

Pizza Florentine (Spring, 33)

Pumpkin-Encrusted Chicken Parmesan (Autumn, 128)

Pumpkin Sage Ravioli (Autumn, 130)
Roast Duck with Orange Sauce (Winter, 173)
Seared Ahi Tuna (Spring, 35)
Sirloin Steak with Herb Butter and Egg (Summer, 87)
Spicy Shrimp Cocktail (Summer, 86)

SIDE DISHES

Artichokes with Red Pepper Aioli (Spring, 40)
Blistered Eggplant with Mozzarella (Summer, 91)
Brussels Sprouts with Butternut Squash and Pecans
    (Winter, 179)
Bourbon Glazed Carrots (Winter, 180)
Corn Bread "Soufflé" (Summer, 93)
Cranberry Sauce (Autumn, 140)
Garlic Cheese Knots (Winter, 178)
Glazed Honey Shrimp Skewers (Spring, 43)
Green Beans with Almonds (Spring, 44)
Pasta Salad with Zucchini, Almonds, and Goat Cheese
    (Summer, 94)
Perfect Guacamole (Summer, 89)
Roasted Red Potatoes with Rosemary (Spring, 45)
Smoked Salmon Carpaccio with Dill, Capers and Quail Eggs
    (Summer, 92)
Spaghetti Squash Roasted in Walnut Olive Oil, Garlic, and
    Parsley (Autumn, 136)
Spiced Sweet Potatoes (Autumn, 134)
Stuffed Mushrooms (Spring, 42)
Sweet Potatoes with Goat Cheese & Bourbon Candied
    Pecan Relish (Autumn, 138)
Warm Southern Corn Bread (Winter, 181)

DESSERTS

Banana Pudding (Summer, 104)
Blueberry Balsamic Gelato (Summer, 100)
Candied Pears (Dipped in Dark Chocolate & Chopped
    Pecans) (Autumn, 142)
Chocolate Azteca Hot Chocolate (Spicy Hot Chocolate)
    (Winter, 183)
Chocolate Cake with Red Wine Pears (Autumn, 145)
Coconut Date Balls (Winter, 187)
Fruit Salad with Blood Orange Olive Oil and Blueberry
    Balsamic Dressing (Summer, 96)

Fruit Salad Bake with Curry (Spring, 58)
Glazed Tarte aux Baies (French Berry Tart) (Spring, 52)
Key Lime Cheesecake Tarts (Summer, 102)
Lemon Cake with Lemon Buttercream Icing (Spring, 47)
Orangettes: Dark-Chocolate-Covered Orange Peels
    (Winter, 186)
Poached Pears with Mint (Autumn, 144)
Pomegranate Christmas Cake with Snow-White Cream
    Cheese Icing (Winter, 184)
Pumpkin Spice Bread Pudding (Autumn, 147)
Raspberry Almond Cream Cheese Tartlets (Summer, 98)
Strawberry Pavlova with Chocolate (Spring, 50)
Strawberry Cake with Strawberry Buttercream Frosting
    (Spring, 55)
Stuffed Baked Apples with Rum (Autumn, 150)
White Chocolate Rocky Road (Winter, 182)

LAGNIAPPE

Abita Molasses Beer Bread (Winter, 194)
Absinthe, the New Orleans way (Spring, 63)
Any Season Crumble with Apricots and Almonds
    (Summer, 106)
Apple Ginger Ale Cocktail (Autumn, 155)
Bananas Foster Croissant French Toast (Spring, 61)
Boudin, Sundried Tomato, and Spinach Omelet
    (Autumn, 151)
Cajun-Spiced Pumpkin Seeds (Autumn, 156)
Cheesy Southern Biscuits (Autumn, 153)
Ciabatta Bread with Cheese, Garlic, and Herbs
    (Winter, 192)
Holiday Eggnog (Winter, 190)
Holiday Pomtini Cocktail (Winter, 191)
Hot Spiced Cider with Rum (Autumn, 154)
Lemon Lavender Muffins (Spring, 66)
Louisiana Lemonade with Several Variations,
    including Pomegranate and Strawberry Lemonade,
    and Limeade (Summer, 111)
Louisiana Bloody Marys (Summer, 109)
Savory Crêpes Boudin (Spring, 59)
Southern Mint Julep (Spring, 65)
Watermelon Feta Salad Cakes (Summer, 113)
Watermelon Juice with Basil (Summer, 107)
Wild Mushroom Onion Quiche (Winter, 189)